THE NEWCASTLE DIOCESAN GAZETTEER A GUIDE TO THE ANGLICAN CHURCHES IN NEWCASTLE UPON TYNE AND NORTHUMBERLAND

Edited by

STANLEY PRINS

ROGER MASSINGBERD-MU...

Published by the Newcastle Diocesan Bishop's Editorial Committee of THE LINK as a contribution to the Diocesan Centenary 1982.

© Newcastle Diocesan Bishop's Editorial Committee
Church House, Grainger Park Road
Newcastle upon Tyne NE4 8SX   April 1982

Printed by Campbell Graphics Ltd
Hawick Crescent Industrial Estate, Newcastle upon Tyne NE6 1AS

ISBN 0 902080 01 6

Acknowledgements

(The LINK Editorial Committee acknowledges the enormous debt that it owes to the clergy of the Diocese of Newcastle, the Stewardship Secretaries, the proof readers and to many others for the help, advice and encouragement that they have given and which has made the production of this book possible.

S. V. Prins: Editor, THE LINK
The Newcastle Diocesan News)

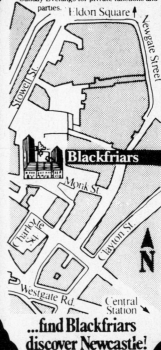

CONTENTS

Saint Michael and All Angels, Newburn.

Foreword by the Rt. Revd. Alec Graham
Lord Bishop of Newcastle

The celebration of the centenary of this diocese will, I hope, make us more aware both of our identity as a diocese and also of our responsibilities to the wider world in which we are set. This gazetteer, which has been prepared by the LINK as its contribution to the celebrations, will certainly help us towards the former end and help to make us aware of the rich variety of church buildings in this diocese. We all have our favourite churches, and no doubt this gazetteer will help us to discover more churches and make us want to add some of them to our list of favourites. As, gazetteer in hand, we make our way from church to church in town and country, we shall be much helped by the introductory essays written by Miss Ridley, Canon Hinkley and Canon Wilson. So, good luck as you set out to discover more of the riches which we have inherited from the past, and I hope that your visits to these churches will move you to reflection on the Church's task in tomorrow's world.

Alec Newcastle

Cathedral Church of St. Nicholas.

OUR LIVING HERITAGE

At a time when the Diocese of Newcastle was still part of the Diocese of Durham an Archdeacon of Northumberland, whose sphere of authority covered the whole of the county from which he derived his title, produced a somewhat daunting report of his Visitation of the parishes. The picture he painted was one of decay and decline. A great many of the churches he had visited were in a serious state of disrepair, and no fewer than eighteen of them, he said, were positively ruinous.

Archdeacons' Visitations nowadays do not produce such depressing reports. Despite inflation and all that makes it increasingly costly to maintain them, our churches — some very old; some very large — are nevertheless, with very few exceptions, in good shape. The Faculty Jurisdiction Measure which brought Diocesan Advisory Committees into being has played its part in helping to uphold good standards both of care and maintenance. Perhaps even more significantly the Inspection of Churches Measure has alerted PCCs regularly to the state of the fabric in their care, and in so doing has arrested any tendency to allow churches to drift almost unnoticed into disrepair. Finding the money to carry out the recommendations arising from an architect's quinquennial inspection is never easy, and for some the operation of vandals, particularly in the theft of roofing lead, has produced an extra burden. But parishes have responded well. Some have been able to qualify for help from the Historic Churches Preservation Trust. In association with this national body and to promote its aims in the Dioceses of Newcastle and Durham we have recently established the Northumbria Historic Churches Trust which hopes to attract contributions and to disburse grants. In the last two years or so further help has been forthcoming from the Department of the Environment which has at last got round to recognising that some parish churches are a sufficiently distinguished part of our national heritage to merit help from public funds towards the cost of their major repairs.

Craftsmen

In all of these ways we must hope that we shall have the ability to be good stewards of this precious inheritance — our parish churches which reflect in their fabric and furnishings the craftsmanship of more than a thousand years. The reader who scans the pages of this useful and informative Gazetteer (and even more those who set out to see for themselves) will soon realize that this diocese is well endowed with fine examples of the skill of ecclesiastical planning, building and furnishing.

The inroads of Scottish raiders which brought destruction to many original churches, especially in the northern part of the diocese, have nevertheless left us with important survivals of Saxon work, especially in the Tyne Valley at Ovingham, Bywell, Corbridge and Warden. The fine churches of Norham and Warkworth reflect Norman work, which is also to be found on a smaller scale at Heddon, Bolam, and Old Bewick (a charmingly restored chapel in the Parish of Eglingham). The observant traveller will find worthy examples from every period up to the present day when, within the inevitable limitations of economic stringency, architects have nevertheless designed new churches which combine practicality with simple dignity. On the way he will not have failed to note the 'grand' churches of the fourteenth and fifteenth centuries at Alnwick, St. John Newcastle, and, of course, the Parish Church of St. Nicholas Newcastle which fell so naturally into the role of Cathedral when the diocese was formed. (Nor will he miss Hexham which might well have done so.)

But I must resist the temptation to embark on a historical survey of the church architecture of the diocese. A perusal of the following pages will soon reveal that from Blanchland Abbey in the south to Berwick, with its Cromwellian church, in the north there is much to be seen.

Features

There will be some, of course, whose interest is not so much in buildings as in their contents and particular design-features. Remarkable historic treasures and objects of beauty are to be found sometimes in the most unlikely and out-of-the-way places. One thinks of the kilted Wise Men carved in Kirknewton Church; the Roman columns at Chollerton; the ancient armour preserved at Delaval; the fine font at Ingram; the Long Pack Grave at Bellingham; the Grey tomb at Chillingham, and the magnificent Ogle tomb at Bothal; Earsdon's Tudor glass brought there from Hampton Court, the distinctively leaded windows at Whittingham and Elsdon, and some good examples of modern glass at Alnmouth and Blyth St. Mary. But again the list is almost endless. Those who journey with the aid of this Gazetteer around our Northumberland churches will find that there is something of special interest almost everywhere.

Worship

But the reader will not, one hopes, fail to note what is perhaps the most significant feature of this work: the schedule of Sunday services for each church. Whatever our architectural, antiquarian, or aesthetic interest may be, our churches are not to be seen primarily as tourist attractions or repositories of fine treasures. They are what they always have been: hallowed places where worship is offered to Almighty God week-by-week. In the fellowship of those times of worship – equally in quiet villages and in the more crowded churches of the city – the visitor is always welcome.

W. T. HINKLEY
*(Chairman of the Northumbria Historic
Churches Trust and of the Diocesan Advisory
Committee for the Care of Churches)*

THE CRADLE OF CHRISTIANITY

The most northerly county in England – Northumberland, can justly claim the title of 'Cradle of Christianity' in the Northern Province. Until the unification of the kingdoms under the Saxons, Northumberland stretched from the Humber to the Forth, ruled by the Kings of Northumbria, one of whom, Edwin gave his name to Scotland's capital Edinburgh. Therefore to be logical the unfortunate designation of the county and official organisations as Northumbria (which the writer refuses to use), which originated during the boundary changes in 1974, and the creation of artificial counties such as Tyne and Wear, was the decision of someone who had never studied history.

Before the impact of the Christian missionaries, the kingdom was largely inhabited by heathens, many of them opposed to the teachings of the intrepid men who penetrated to their wild northern kingdom. It was the early Queens-Consort who influenced their husbands and converted them to the Christian faith. This faith prompted King Oswald to send for a man whose name in the history of the Church is immortal. From the little island of Iona, off the west coast of Scotland came a man named Aidan, a friend of Oswald, who preached and converted many Northumbrians. St. Aidan (he was subsequently canonised), settled on the island of Lindisfarne, which lies close to the 'lordly strand of Northumberland', and is now known throughout the Christian world as Holy Island. Lindisfarne was then part of Bamburghshire, its mighty fortress, Bamburgh Castle dominates the coast to this day.

Aidan

It is recorded that the man from Iona had difficulty in understanding the Northumbrian speech and had to rely on an interpreter! This is not surprising as the varying dialects of Northumberland present a problem to the stranger today. St. Aidan and his followers laid the foundations of the Priory Church on Holy Island. Now ruined but magnificent, it has an atmosphere of sanctity and continuity. The close by Church of St. Mary which is the parish church dates partly from the twelfth century. Appropriately Northumberland has two Archdeacons, one bearing the name of the county, the other that of Lindisfarne.

King Oswald who brought St. Aidan to his kingdom, deserves the description of the 'rocker of the cradle'. In 633 the King achieved a great victory at the Battle of Heavenfield (near Wall), over the heathen forces of the Welsh King Cadwalla. A wooden cross at the top of Brunton Bank on the Military Road marks the spot where it is reputed the Christian King prayed before the battle. Oswald died in 642 in a battle against another heathen, Penda of Mercia, near Oswestry. He was a hero, deserving the title saint, whose veneration spread to many parts of Europe.

Cuthbert

After the death of St. Aidan in 651, the light still burnt brightly in the North and many followed in the footsteps of the Saint; one of whom was to become the most greatly loved and most vividly remembered; a shepherd laddie whose name was Cuthbert. Watching the sheep on Dod Law, a hill in Glendale which overlooks the little town of Wooler, the boy had a vision in which he saw the angels bearing St. Aidan to heaven in their arms. Cuthbert decided that he would devote his life to the preaching of the Gospel, first studying for a time at Melrose under St. Eata. In 684, at the invitation of King Egbert he accepted the bishopric of Hexham. Very shortly after he exchanged this Bishopric with that of Eata at Lindisfarne where he spent the rest of his comparatively short life, teaching, preaching and counselling, before dying on the Inner Farne in 687 famed as a worker of miracles and for the beauty of his holiness.

With the coming of the Norsemen the monks carried his coffin, some say for two hundred years, resting at some of the many churches from Northumberland to Yorkshire until a resting place was found for him where the mighty cathedral of Durham stands today; the finest Norman cathedral in Europe. Many of the churches where the Saint's body rested are dedicated to his memory. Cuthbert, as described by the Venerable Bede, appears to have been a very human saint. He loved birds and today on Holy Island some breeds are known as his 'chicks'. Tiny round pebbles are St. Cuthbert's beads. His memory will never die.

Another saint who has written his name of the pages of Northumbrian history is Paulinus, famous for his 'mass' baptisms. Tradition has it that thousands of people were received into the Church at Pallinsburn, on the Wooler road, at The Lady's or St. Ninian's Well at Holystone in Coquetdale and, some say, on the Roman Wall north of Haltwhistle! There must have been many 'back-sliders' and the county's history, until the Union of the English and Scottish Crowns, was a wild and turbulent one. Yet in those violent days the faith was strong and a future Marian martyr Nicholas Ridley was Christened in St. Cuthbert's Church at Beltingham.

In this centenary year of the Bishopric of Newcastle we remember with love and praise these men who built the 'cradle'; may we follow in their example. I end this inadequate appreciation with the last verse of the 13th chapter of Corinthians:

> "And now abideth faith, hope, and charity, these three;
> but the greatest of these is charity."

Nancy Ridley

(Nancy Ridley is the author of several books on Northumberland.)

THE DIOCESE OF NEWCASTLE 1882-1982

The County of Northumberland with Berwick on Tweed, though anciently a part of the great diocese of Durham, was a distinctive region, with its own character and traditions. Within its borders is situated Lindisfarne, the illustrious centre of mission for the North of England and beyond.

Industrial Growth

Proposals to form a new diocese in the sixteenth century came to nothing, possibly for good reasons, since the motives are not altogether clear. When, a hundred years ago, the present diocese was founded, it was not simply to revive memories of Northumberland's brilliant past. It was, on the contrary, inaugurated as part of the Church's response to an urgent, contemporary need. This need was to provide more adequate pastoral care for the vastly increased populations which had sprung up in the great new industrial areas of England, and which were largely unchurched.

Churches Response

This response was tardy rather than premature: when it was made, it was appropriate that the new diocese should have its symbolic centre in the midst of a great industrial city. This endeavour to meet the circumstances of the time implied no unawareness of the past, or of the abiding rural nature of most of its area; quite the contrary. One of the aspects of diocesan history which should be remembered with gratitude is the way in which any untoward tension between town and country, industry and agriculture has been avoided.

Past and Future

No small part of this is due to the good fortune of the new diocese in its first Bishop. He had much to do with the successful beginnings of the diocesan story, and this is an age when circumstances were far from easy. Then was strengthened and built up a family diocesan feeling which endures to this day, nurtured and sustained by Ernest Wilberforce's successors. The hundred years have seen many vicissitudes in Northumberland as in the whole world. In 1982 there is much cause for gratitude in the story which has unfolded. Christians must have faith in the past as well as in the future. In gratitude and recognition of what has gone before, we make our centenary a celebration which may dare to face the future because of what we know of the past.

Andrew Wilson,
Canon of the Cathedral Church
of St. Nicholas, Newcastle upon Tyne

THE DEANERIES
The Archdeaconry of Northumberland

NEWCASTLE CENTRAL DEANERY –

Dinnington, St. Matthew
        St. Cuthbert, Brunswick Village
Epiphany Team, St. Mary the Virgin, Fawdor
        St. Hugh, Gosforth
        The Epiphany, Kingston
        Park
Gosforth, All Saints
Gosforth, St. Nicholas
Kenton, The Church of the Ascension
Woodlands Park, St. Chad
        St. Aidan, Brunton Park
Newcastle, Cathedral Church of St. Nicholas
        St. Andrew, Newgate St.
        St. Ann, City Road
        Christ Church, Shieldfield
        St. John the Baptist, Grainger St.
        St. Luke, Spital Tongues
        St. Thomas the Martyr, Barras
        Bridge
        Holy Trinity, Jesmond
        Parish Church, Jesmond
        St. George, Jesmond
        St. Hilda, Jesmond
        St. Barnabas' and St. Jude,
        Sandyford

NEWCASTLE EAST DEANERY –

Byker, St. Mark
Byker, St. Martin
Byker, St. Michael
Byker, St. Silas
Heaton, St. Gabriel
Heaton, St. Francis
Benton, St. Bartholomew
Longbenton, St. Mary Magdalen
Walker, Christ Church
Walker, St. Anthony of Egypt
Walkergate, St. Oswald

NEWCASTLE WEST DEANERY –

Inner West

Benwell, St. James
        Venerable Bede
        St. John the Baptist, Benwell Village

Cowgate, St. Peter
Fenham, Holy Cross
Fenham, St. Augustine
Fenham, St. James and St. Basil
High Elswick, St. Paul
High Elswick, St. Philip
Low Elswick, St. Stephen
Newcastle, St. Matthew
Scotswood, St. Margaret

Outer West

Denton, Church of the Holy Spirit
Newburn, St. Michael and All Angels
        St. Cuthbert, Blucher
        St. Mary, Throckley
        Holy Trinity, Dalton
Ponteland, St. Mary the Virgin
        Holy Saviour, Milbourne
Sugley, Holy Saviour
Whorlton Team Ministry, Church of the Holy
        Nativity, Chapel
        House
        St. Wilfrid,
        Newbiggin Hall
        St. John, Whorlton

TYNEMOUTH DEANERY –

Balkwell, St. Peter
Cullercoats Team, St. Aidan, Billy Mill
        St. George, Cullercoats
        St. Hilda, Marden
Earsdon, St. Alban
        St. John the Baptist, Backworth
Monkseaton, St. Mary the Virgin
Monkseaton, St. Peter
North Shields, Christ Church
        (Tynemouth Parish Church)
        St. Augustin
Percy Main, St. John
Shiremoor, St. Mark
Tynemouth Priory, Holy Saviour
Wallsend, St. John the Evangelist
Wallsend, St. Luke
Wallsend, St. Peter
Whitley Bay, St. Paul
Willington Team, St. Mary the Virgin,
        Willington
        St. Paul the Apostle,
        Willington Quay (Howdon)
        Church of the Good
        Shepherd, Battle Hill

The Archdeaconry of Lindisfarne

ALNWICK DEANERY — Pages 91-100

Alnmouth, St. John the Baptist
St. Mary, Lesbury
Alnwick, St. Michael
Bolton Chapel
St. John the Baptist, Edlingham
Alwinton, St. Michael and All Angels
St. Michael and All Angels, Alnham
St. Mary the Virgin, Holystone
Amble, St. Cuthbert
Chevington, St. John the Divine
Embleton, The Holy Trinity
St. Peter the Fisherman, Craster
All Saints, Rennington
St. Philip and St. James, Rock
Village
Newton by the Sea, Mission Church
Felton, St. Michael and all Angels
Longframlington, St. Mary the Virgin
St. Peter and St. Paul,
Brinkburn Priory
Longhoughton, St. Peter and St. Paul
St. Andrew, Boulmer
St. Michael and All Angels,
Howick
Rothbury, All Saints
Christ Church, Hepple
St. Andrew, Thropton
Shilbotle, St. James
Warkworth, St. Lawrence
St. John the Divine, Acklington
Whittingham, St. Bartholomew
St. Peter, Glanton

BAMBURGH DEANERY — Pages 103-108

Bamburgh, St. Aidan
St. Hilda, Lucker
Beadnell, St. Ebba
St. Maurice, Ellingham
Belford, St. Mary
North Sunderland, St. Paul
Wooler Group of Parishes,
St. Mary, Wooler
Holy Cross, Chatton
St. Peter, Chillingham
St. Mary and St. Michael, Doddington
St. Maurice, Eglingham
St. Michael, Ilderton
St. Michael and All Angels, Ingram
St. Gregory, Kirknewton
Holy Trinity, Old Bewick
St. James, South Charlton

MORPETH DEANERY — Pages 111-120

Ashington, Holy Sepulchre
St. Aidan, Linton
Bothal, St. Andrew
Hartburn, St. Andrew
St. John the Baptist, Meldon
St. Giles, Netherwitton
Kirkwhelpington, St. Bartholomew
Holy Trinity, Cambo
St. Wilfrid, Kirkharle
St. Bartholomew,
Kirkheaton
Longhirst, John the Evangelist
St. Cuthbert, Hebron
Longhorsley, St. Helen
Lynemouth, St. Aidan
St. Bartholomew, Cresswell
Mitford, St. Mary Magdalene
Morpeth, St. James the Great
St. Mary the Virgin
St. Aidan, Stobhill
Seaton Hirst, St. Andrew
St. John the Evangelist
Ulgham, St. John the Baptist
The Holy Trinity, Widdrington
St. Mary, Widdrington Station
Whalton, St. Mary Magdalene
St. Andrew, Bolam
Woodhorn, St. Mary the Virgin
St. Bartholomew, Newbiggin by
the Sea

NORHAM DEANERY — Pages 123-128

Berwick, St. Mary
Holy Trinity
Cornhill on Tweed, St. Helen
St. Paul, Branxton
St. Cuthbert, Carham
Ford, St. Michael and All Angels
St. Mary the Virgin, Etal
Holy Island, St. Mary the Virgin
Lowick, St. John the Baptist
St. Nicholas, Kyloe
Norham, St. Cuthbert
All Saints, Duddo
Spittal, St. John the Evangelist
St. Anne Ancroft
Tweedmouth, St. Bartholomew
St. Peter, Scremerston

St. Mary the Virgin, Stannington.

BEDLINGTON DEANERY

St. Cuthbert's Church, Bedlington
Consecrated circa AD 900
St. Cuthberts is the ancient parish church of Bedlingtonshire; until the last century, part of the Palatinate County of Durham. Small traces of Saxon and Norman work survive.

The body of St. Cuthbert rested here on 12 December 1069, during the wanderings prior to his interment at Durham. The church was enlarged in 1910 by the addition of a north aisle. The great window at its western end commemorates Squire Burdon, last Squire of Humford, and it includes the proof of Pythagoras' theorem.

The south porch (c.1350) is a memorial chapel to the dead of the World Wars and records the names of over 400 local miners who perished then.
Times of Sunday Services:
8.30 a.m. Holy Communion
9.30 a.m. Choral Eucharist
6.00 p.m. Evensong
Telephone: Vicarage – Bedlington 823212
Road Location: Church Lane, Bedlington.

St. Cuthbert's Church, Blyth
Consecrated in 1885
The original church or chapel of ease of this parish was a simple and unpretentious building erected in 1751 on a site now occupied by the parish hall. The present church, is a stately and dignified structure of stone in a cruciform style with a fine battlement tower housing a chiming clock, which was presented in 1962 as a memorial gift by George Colpitts.

The association with the old church has been preserved by incorporating some of its possessions into the new church. Communion plate, dated, 1762, given by the Ridley family is still in use. The bell used for more than 100 years in the old church was transferred and hung in the new tower.
Times of Sunday Services:
8.00 a.m. Holy Communion (said)
9.45 a.m. Parish Communion (sung)
6.00 p.m. Evensong
Telephone: Vicarage – Blyth 2410
Road Location: Wellington Street, Plessey Road, Blyth.

St. Mary's Church, Blyth
Consecrated in 1864

St. Mary's was built as a chapel of ease in the parish of Horton in 1864 by Austin and Johnson, and consisted of a chancel, nave and south porch. The parish was formed in 1897. A north aisle was added as well as extensions to the chancel and west end by W. S. Hicks 1897-1903. The aisle contains the Lady Altar where the Blessed Sacrament is reserved. The font, designed by G. E. Charlewood about 1936 for the now redundant church of St. Lawrence Byker, was removed to St. Mary's in 1979. The high altar candlesticks were designed by L. C. Evetts, as well as windows in the aisles of St. Aidan and St. Cuthbert. The large crucifix in the church grounds came from a bombed London church.

Times of Sunday Services:
7.30 a.m. Mattins
8.00 a.m. Holy Communion
9.45 a.m. Sung Eucharist
6.00 p.m. Evensong
Times of daily offices and eucharist on the notice board in church.
Telephone: Vicarage – Blyth 3417
Road Location: At the west end of Blyth market.

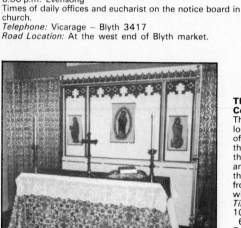

The Good Shepherd, Burradon
Consecrated in 1894

The entrance to the church, which is situated behind the local school, is marked by a large cross. This cross is made of Australian hardwood which was taken from the shaft of the local colliery just after its closure in 1975. It stands therefore as a reminder of the colliery which 'used to be' and of the church which is still with us. The interior shows three tapestries which were originally panels of an altar frontal presented to the church in its very early days. These will be at least 100 years old.

Times of Sunday Services:
10.00 a.m. Holy Communion and Children's Instruction
 6.00 p.m. Evening Prayer
Telephone: Priest in Charge – Newcastle 500698
Road Location: Burradon Village.

St. Andrew's Church, Cambois
Consecrated in 1898

The daughter church of Cambois parish situated quite near to the coast. Its community has been reduced in latter years by rehousing schemes and the closure of local industry.

Times of Sunday Services:
10.00 a.m. Sunday Eucharist alternately with St. Peter's
 5.15 p.m. each Sunday with fortnightly evening Eucharist
Telephone: Vicarage – Bedlington 822309
Road Location: Adjacent to Blyth Power Station.

St. Peter's Church, West Sleekburn, Cambois
Consecrated in 1867

The parish of Cambois was originally part of St. Cuthbert's, Bedlington. The closure of the local colliery and the reduction of housing has left a small community, served by the vicar of Sleekburn and a non-stipendiary priest.

Times of Sunday Services:
10.00 a.m. Sunday Eucharist alternately with St. Andrew's
6.15 p.m. Eucharist on the intervening Sundays
Telephone: Vicarage – Bedlington 822309
Road Location: Bedlington to Cambois road.

St. Paul the Apostle, Choppington
Consecrated in 1866

A small unpretentious 'colliery church', it was built to serve the growing mining village of Choppington. Architecturally it is simple and uncluttered, set in a spacious churchyard containing some fine beech trees. The processional cross is in memory of those who lost their lives in the two Choppington pits – both closed in the early 1960s. The brass altar cross is of unusual design and of particularly fine workmanship. Once a colliery church, St. Paul's now serves a parish of several large housing estates.

Times of Sunday Services:
  8.00 a.m. Mattins
10.30 a.m. Sung Eucharist
  5.00 p.m. Evensong
Telephone: Vicarage – Bedlington 822216
Road Location: On the A1068, approximately 1 mile north of Bedlington.

Church of the Holy Family, Choppington, Stakeford
Dedicated in 1962

This is a dual purpose building of simple, modern design. Mercifully free from the architectural flights of fancy that were all too common in the 1960s, e.g. expanses of glass, electrical under floor heating etc. The Church of the Holy Family is a highly practical piece of parish equipment serving the estates which run either side of Stakeford Lane. The building is also well-equipped to serve as a church hall, with storerooms, a good sized kitchen, meeting room and toilets.

Times of Sunday Services:
The principal service is the 9.00 a.m. Eucharist
Telephone: Vicarage – Bedlington 822216
Road Location: Go through Choppington to Stakeford roundabout (junction of A196 with A1068) turn right, $\frac{1}{2}$ mile down on the left.

19

St. Benedict, Cowpen
Consecrated in 1961

Dual purpose building built to serve post war housing development in Cowpen and Bebside.
Time of Sunday Service:
10.00 a.m. Sung Mass
Telephone: Vicarage – Bedlington 823297
Road Location: Leave Cowpen Road (main road Blyth to Bebside) by Tynedale Drive, Brierly Road is ninth turning on left.

St. Nicholas' Church, Cramlington
Consecrated in 1868

By 1270 Cramlington is said to have had a chapel. This was served by Chaplains from the Mother Church in Newcastle. It follows then that this Church eventually took the name St. Nicholas. The present church was built in response to rapid increases in the population in the middle of the nineteenth century resulting from the growth of coal mining. The Cramlington area had six pits. The mining industry died, and now the Church-in-the-Village is an important piece of history at the heart of Northumberland's New Town.

It has a peal of six bells.
Times of Sunday Services:
8.00 a.m. Holy Communion
9.15 a.m. Parish Communion
6.00 p.m. Evening Prayer or Communion
Telephone: Vicarage.– 0670 712259
Road Location: Cramlington Village (adjacent to Cramlington New Town Centre).

Our Lady's Church, Delaval
Consecrated in 1102

Taken out of Parish of Earsdon in 1891 to form new Parish of Delaval. Previously private chapel of Delaval family with access to inhabitants of Manor. Built by Hubert Delaval and consecrated in 1102. Retains original Norman features of nave, choir and presbytery divided by distinctive moulded arches with zigzag and billet ornamentations. Other features include thirteenth century effigies of knight and lady, eight cusped panels containing shields bearing Delaval and other arms dating from fourteenth century, original trefoiled opening in Presbytery containing piscina bowl with credence shelf above, hatchments of later Delaval and Hastings families and fine eighteenth century ceiling in nave.
Times of Sunday Services:
8.00 a.m. Holy Communion
6.15 p.m. Evensong (3rd and 5th Sundays)
Telephone: Vicarage – Seaton Delaval 371982
Road Location: Between Seaton Delaval and Seaton Sluice, Church located to the rear of Seaton Delaval Hall.

St. Paul's Church, Seaton Sluice, Delaval
Consecrated in 1961

Daughter church in the parish of Delaval, converted from a former community hall for use as a church in 1961. Although not purpose-built it was somewhat ahead of its time in that it is well equipped with separate meeting hall, chapel, vestry and kitchen. St. Paul's cannot be said to be of any special architectural or historic interest, but its position close to an attractive harbour, fine dunes and beach, wooded country walks, and easy access from the city – not to mention the above facilities – make it sought after for day retreats by urban parishes.

Times of Sunday Services:
10.00 a.m. Holy Communion
 6.15 p.m. Evensong (1st Sunday in month)
Telephone: Vicarage – Seaton Delaval 371982
Road Location: On the sea front, Beresford Road.

St. Paul's Church, Dudley
Dedicated in 1886

St. Paul's, Dudley, was built as a mission chapel of Killingworth and dedicated in 1886 by Bishop Wilberforce. The district had been known as Weetslade (vale of the willows) until the Dudley Pit, named after the owner's son, opened in 1854 and gave its name to the village. The parish was created in 1970 taking in parts of Killingworth, North Gosforth and Seghill.

Since the closure of the pit in 1977, the parish has become a residential area, most of its workers travelling to Tyneside.

Times of Sunday Services:
8.30 a.m. Mattins (said)
9.00 a.m. Parish Communion – sung
6.00 p.m. Evensong (said)
Telephone: Vicarage – Newcastle 500251
Road Location: Between North Gosforth and Cramlington off the old A1.

St. Mary's Church, Holywell
Consecrated in 1885

Built to a design by W. S. Hicks, on a site gifted by the Rev. J. E. E. Bates, with other sites for a priest's house, and church hall. Originally a chapel of ease within Earsdon parish, and created a Conventional District during 1940s. Parochial boundary changes placed Holywell within Seghill and Seaton Delaval Parish in 1957. Shortage of parish funds, and reduction in Diocesan complement of assistant clergy, has resulted in there being no Priest-in-Charge since the middle of the 1960s.

Times of Sunday Services:
8.00 a.m. Holy Communion (said)
6.00 p.m. Currently joint worship with Methodist/URC at Elsdon Ave. Methodist/URC site
Telephone: Vicarage – Seaton Delaval 371601
Road Location: On A192 Seaton Delaval, to Holywell and Earsdon road.

St. Mary the Virgin, Horton
Date of consecration unknown. Church of 12th century foundation. Rebuilt 1827, restored 1900
Church at Horton administered by Prior of Tynemouth in 1147. 1650 Church Commissioners recommended erection into Parish, including Blyth Neuk, Newsham and Cramlington. 1768 finally separated from Woodhorn.

Memorial stone in south wall to Anne Barbowle. Bell dated 1621. Eighteenth century sun dial. 1903 restoration by Hicks of Newcastle.

Times of Sunday Services:
8.30 a.m. Sung Mass
4.00 p.m. Sung Evensong
Telephone: Vicarage – Bedlington 823297
Road Location: A192 between Ashington spine road (A189) and Bedlington. Quarter of a mile from spine road intersection.

The Church of the Holy Family, Killingworth
Consecrated in 1974
A shared church built and maintained by the Killingworth Christian Council. There is an ecumenical congregation and a Roman Catholic congregation.

Being part of the Communicare Centre the church is open throughout the week. The Warden of Communicare Team Ministry co-ordinates professional and voluntary staff. He is also the Anglican priest.

People seeking experience of ministry or in need of help are accommodated at Communicare House in Angus Close or the annexe in Hebburn Tower.

Times of Sunday Services:
9.45 a.m. Ecumenical Worship
6.00 p.m. Ecumenical Worship
11.15 a.m. Roman Catholic Mass
4.00 p.m. Baptisms (2nd and 4th Sundays)
Telephone: Communicare House – 681497
Church Office – 683667
Road Location: Communicare Centre, Killingworth Township.

St. John the Envangelist, Killingworth
Consecrated in 1869
Designed by Bassett Keeling of London, and faced with local stone, with bands of pink sandstone from a local quarry. It stands in beautiful grounds in the old village of Killingworth, surrounded by elm and sycamore trees. It is a popular church ministering to a wide age-group and particularly welcoming to young families. A special children's room is available with all facilities during services.

Times of Sunday Services:
8.00 a.m. Holy Communion (1st Sunday only)
9.15 a.m. Parish Communion (except 1st Sunday)
10.00 a.m. Family Communion (1st Sunday only)
6.00 p.m. Evensong (2nd Sunday)
Telephone: Vicarage – 0632 683242
Road Location: B1317 at OS NZ 279710 in Killingworth Village.

St. Michael and All Angels, New Hartley
Consecrated in 1900

New Hartley came into existence with the sinking of the fated Hester Pit in 1845, and a small wooden church was built by the Parish of Earsdon to be replaced in 1900 by a church designed by J. Dobinson of the Seaton Delaval Coal Company. The colleries and their rows of cottages have long since disappeared, but still in the centre of an ever-growing village is the church of 'red brick with stone capping' and 'a commodius vestry' (*Newcastle Diocesan Gazette*, Sept. 1900). It is kept open for private prayer and the visitor will be impressed with its excellent state of repair.

Times of Sunday Services:
9.00 a.m. Parish Communion
11.15 a.m. Junior Church
6.15 p.m. Evensong (2nd and 4th Sundays)
Telephone: Vicarage – Seaton Delaval 371150
Road Location: St. Michael's Ave., New Hartley, Whitley Bay NE25 0RP.

St. Bede's Church, Newsham
Consecrated in 1957

An attractive, brick built modern church serving the former mining village of Newsham and New Delaval. Though now part of Blyth, Newsham retains its character and the church has constantly been a part of the life of the community. As the population has moved so the church has moved, this present building being the fourth and most permanent. Small and compact it ideally suits contemporary trends of worship, bringing together the worshipper and celebrant in an atmosphere of sacramental family worship.

Times of Sunday Services:
8.00 a.m. Holy Communion
9.00 a.m. Parish Communion
11.00 a.m. Children
6.00 p.m. Evensong
Telephone: Vicarage – Blyth 2391
Road Location: Newcastle Road, Blyth.

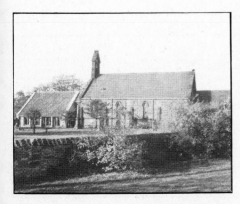

The Holy Trinity, Seghill
Consecrated in 1849

Building to a design by Benjamin and John Green, architects of a number of important buildings in Newcastle during Grainger/Dobson era, although Holy Trinity has no special features. Notable ministry from the Reverend Charles Osborne, D. D. over the turn of the century. He was a disciple of the Tractarians and in consequence persecuted by the Ecclesiastical Commission on Discipline. (Osborne was the author of recognised works on Pastoralia for the clergy, and a biographer of some of the Tractarians disciples.)

Broadly Catholic tradition. Extensions in 1981.

Times of Sunday Services:
9.15 a.m. Sung Eucharist
6.00 p.m. Currently joint worship with Methodist/URC at Elsdon Ave. Methodist/URC site
Telephone: Vicarage – Seaton Delaval 371601
Road Location: Off A190 Annitsford to Seaton Delaval road.

St. John the Evangelist, Sleekburn
Consecrated in 1906
Formerly part of St. Cuthbert's, Bedlington. A church built mainly in local brick with interior stone piers. Chancel screen added in recent years.
Times of Sunday Services:
9.30 a.m. Sung Eucharist
6.40 p.m. Evening Prayer (HC on 2nd Sunday)
Telephone: Vicarage – Bedlington 822309
Road Location: North View, Bedlington Station.

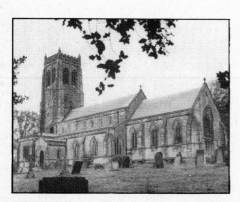

St. Mary the Virgin, Stannington
Original church consecrated in 1190 now demolished
Present church consecrated on 31 October 1871
The pillars on the north side of the nave were embedded in the well of the old church.

Chapiters at east and west of both aisles also come from the old church. There are mediaeval grave covers and possibly one Saxon grave cover (a child of quality) under the tower. There is a window containing mediaeval glass given in 1722 by Sir Matthew White Ridley in the vicar's vestry. There is also a parapet stone from the tower of the old church under the present church tower – the underside of which has the figure of a man dancing and a skull on it.
Times of Sunday Services:
2nd Sunday 9.30 a.m. Mattins
Other Sundays 9.30 a.m. Holy Communion
Evensong 6.00 p.m. summer; 3.00 p.m. winter
Holy Commuion after evensong on 2nd and 3rd Sundays
Road Location: To west of North Road on Church Road, Stannington.

SHEPHERDS DENE RETREAT HOUSE

The House was built as a private residence at the turn of the century and given to the Diocese of Newcastle in 1946 by the Stirling-Newall family. It is set in 20 acres of garden and woodland.

Responsibility for running the house is now shared by the Dioceses of Newcastle and Durham.

Shepherds Dene caters for:

Clergy and Lay retreats

Parish and Deanery weekends
Clergy and lay residential and day meetings
Secular meetings and conference (when the house is not required for church functions).

There is sleeping accommodation for 30 and the chapel can seat up to 40. Each party can use the chapel as required and it is also open to individual visitors.

THE COMMUNITY OF THE HOLY NAME

The Community of the Holy Name was founded by Fr. George Herbert in the Parish of St. Peter, Vauxhall in 1865. The Mother House was later established in Malvern Link. There are community houses in several parts of England and in Africa.

Sisters of the Community have had a house in Newcastle for twenty years and in 1981 moved to a house in Walker. They are chiefly engaged in parish work.

The Community lives to a rule and the focal point of their way of life is prayer and intercession. There is a small chapel in their house in Walker.

Some of the parishes in the City will know the value of their work. They carry out engagements in other parts of the Diocese from time to time.

Telephone: Wallsend 624265.

THE SOCIETY OF ST. FRANCIS

The Anglican order of the Society of St. Francis was founded in 1921. Its Mother House is at Cerne Abbess and its Friary houses are to be found in all parts of the world.

The houses are a centre of prayer and the brothers are engaged in teaching and pastoral missions. They live as a community and follow a life-style inspired by St. Francis of Assisi, whose eight hundredth anniversary is celebrated in 1982.

This Diocese is fortunate in having a Friary at Alnmouth. It commands magnificent views across vast stretches of the Northumberland coast line and the Chapel is beautiful in its simplicity.

Visitors are welcome for retreats, quiet days, conferences and courses, or by arrangement.

Telephone: Alnmouth 213.

St. Giles, Birtley.

St. Cuthbert's, Elsdon.

26

BELLINGHAM DEANERY

St. Cuthbert's Church, Bellingham
Year of consecration estimated 1180
Mediaeval font perfectly suited to a small church. The only all stone roof for a church in England, a monument to two burnings in the raiding times added in 1603, plus many buttresses afterwards because of the weight. Outside lies the Long Pack Grave the centre of a brutal Bellingham tale.
Times of Sunday Services:
  8.00 a.m. Holy Communion
11.00 a.m. Holy Communion
  6.00 p.m. Evensong
Telephone: Vicarage – Bellingham 20225
Road Location: Centre of Bellingham.

St. Giles, Birtley
Consecrated in 1090
There was probably a church on this site (which commands a fine view over North Tynedale) in the seventh century, and there is a small memorial stone, almost unique, from this time, now set in the chancel wall. The present church, much (but very well) rebuilt, retains a Norman arch and other early stonework, and has several mediaeval gravestones standing in the porch. A three-sided gravestone behind the church should be noted. There are some fine windows.
Times of Sunday Services;
9.30 a.m. Holy Communion – all Sundays except 2nd
6.30 p.m. Evensong – 2nd Sunday
Telephone: Vicarage – Bellingham 30223
Road Location: About 2 miles east of Wark.

St. Francis' Church, Byrness
Consecrated in 1799

This building was once the smallest in the Diocese situated about ½ a mile from the Village, where the Pennine Way crosses the A68. Formerly a chapel under Elsdon parish but now a separate parish in the Bellingham/Otterburn Group.

Times of Sunday Services:
1st Sunday 3.00 p.m. Evensong
3rd Sunday 9.30 a.m. Holy Communion
Telephone: Vicarage – Otterburn 20212
Road Location: On the A68 ½ mile south of Byrness Village next to Byrness Filling Station and cafe.

St. Giles' Church, Chollerton – Consecrated in 1097

This church was probably built by William de Swinburne, a Scottish Knight about 1260. The gravestone built into the wall of the porch may belong to his wife, Elizabeth; it asks us to pray for her soul. There have been a number of burials within the walls of the Church, one of them being of the local Roman Catholic Priest in 1782.

The present church is built on the site of an earlier Saxon Church served by the Monks of Hexham.

Its great interest to the antiquarians is the arcade of Roman pillars which have been taken from the Roman Camp at Chesters on the other side of the river. The second one from the front shows well the Roman feather-tooling.

Also to be noted is the Roman altar which has been inverted and hollowed out to serve as a font.

Note also organ by Father Schmidt a famous organ builder in the time of Elizabeth I. Windows in south side of the choir dedicated to members of the Bird family who restored the church.

Times of Sunday Services:
10.30 a.m. Holy Communion (1st, 3rd and 5th Sundays)
10.30 a.m. Morning Prayer (2nd and 4th Sundays)
Telephone: Vicarage – Humshaugh 721
Road Location: On main road from Hexham to Rothbury.

St. Cuthbert's Church, Corsenside
Consecrated in 1120

Corsenside, tradition says, was one of the resting places of the monks fleeing from Lindisfarne with Saint Cuthbert's body. The earliest record of the church is dated 1242. The church is of simple, un-ornamented Norman design, the stone quite likely was plundered from the nearby Roman fort Habitancum.

The shape of the chancel arch and the apparent mis-fit of the bell turret have led to speculation that they may have been transported reasonably intact. There is a stone seat of an ancient cross to the south of the church and many interesting grave stones. Inside the church itself are saxon and celtic crosses and a number of interesting features in the stone work. Lovely ancient church well worth visiting.

No regular services
Telephone: Vicarage – West Woodburn 60235
Road Location: ¼ miles from A68 (s.p. Corsenside app. 2 miles north of West Woodburn).

St. Cuthbert's Church, Elsdon

Built about 1400 in the shape of a cross. The church is dedicated to St. Cuthbert whose body is said to have rested here for a short time in 875, during the wanderings of the Monks of Lindisfarne. This church replaced a small Norman building. It is thought that the Vicar's Pele, a fortified parsonage, also dates from about 1400 when plundering by the Scots was particularly bad. Note: on the pillars nearest the entrance are many deep grooves made by the fighting men sharpening their weapons. The only remnants of the Norman church built in 1100 – are two pillars set in west wall and perhaps two small round headed windows.

Times of Sunday Services:
1st Sunday 9.30 a.m. The Eucharist(SIII)
2nd Sunday 8.30 a.m. The Eucharist (BCP)
3rd Sunday 5.15 p.m. Evensong
4th Sunday 9.30 a.m. The Eucharist (S.III)
Telephone: Vicarage – Otterburn 20212
Road Location: Elsdon Village.

St. Peter's Church, Falstone
Consecrated in 1892

Falstone church, situated one mile downstream of the great dam of Kielder Water, was built upon the burned-out remains of its 1824 predecessor. The latter had been the first parish church of Falstone, which had only become a parish in 1811, the whole area having been, previously, part of the Great Parish of Simonburn. A small, unpretentious building remarkable for the great sense of peace within it. In 1981 the URC church in the village closed; since then both congregations have been worshipping together in St. Peter's.

Times of Sunday Services:
10.00 a.m. United Worship, alternating Sunday by Sunday between Communion and a URC service
6.00 p.m. Evening Worship (united) on first Sunday
Telephone: Vicarage – Bellingham 40213
Road Location: 9 miles north of Bellingham on unclassified road to Kielder and Kielder Water, turn right to Falstone ($\frac{1}{2}$ mile), church is on the right behind the Blackcock Inn.

St. Luke's Church
Greystead
Consecrated in 1818

This is another of the Seward churches built in 1818 for the Commissioners of Greenwich Hospital. It resembles Wark, Humshaugh and Thorneyburn. It is surrounded by trees in a secluded position.

Times of Sunday Services
9.00 a.m. Holy Communion (1st Sunday in the month)
3.30 p.m. Evening Prayer (3rd Sunday in the month)
Telephone: Bellingham Vicarage – Bellingham 20225
Road Location: On the C199 between Bellingham and Falstone.

St. Christopher's Church, Gunnerton
Consecrated in 1900

Built in 1899/1900, Mr. John Hawes being the architect (he later became a Roman Catholic monk) and Bishop Hornby being the Vicar at the time. The site was given by Col. Hornby. The church is in the English traditional style and built of rough faced stone. It seats about 100 and originally cost just over £700.

Times of Sunday Services:
9.00 a.m. Holy Communion (1st and 3rd Sundays in month)
Telephone: Chollerton Vicarage — Humshaugh 721
Road Location: Turn right (first turning) on road from Barrasford to Wark.

Holy Trinity Church, Horsley
Consecrated in 1844

The then Lord Redesdale had the church built and endowed the living. It is built high up on the side of a hill overlooking the Rede Valley. It is a pleasant building with fine oak pews and a magnificent reredos behind the altar. In the porch is a Roman altar and several interesting stones that have been unearthed locally.

Times of Sunday Services:
9.30 a.m. Eucharist
Telephone: Vicarage — West Woodburn 60235
Road Location: A68 ¾ mile south of Rochester, 4 miles north of Otterburn.

St. Peter's Church, Humshaugh
Consecrated in 1818

A Georgian church by H. H. Seward, a pupil of Sir John Soane, to replace the chapel long in ruins at Haughton Castle. After the unsuccessful 1745 Jacobite uprising the right of presentation to the parish of Simonburn passed to the Governors of Greenwich Hospital who built this along with Wark, Greystead and Thorneyburn (qv). The building is of hand dressed freestone; tall windows have simple tracery; the Royal Arms (George III) include the cap of the Electors of Hanover; the other arms are of the Greenwich Hospital. The builder is Thomas Nixon of Wall whose grave is in the churchyard by the south wall.

Times of Sunday Services:
9.00 a.m. Holy Communion
10.30 a.m. Family Service
6.30 p.m. Evening Prayer
Telephone: Vicarage — Humshaugh 304
Road Location: Half a mile north of Chollerford Bridge.

St. John the Evangelist, Otterburn
Consecrated approx 1858
The church was once served from Elsdon but now as the main centre of population in Redesdale it is a separate entity within the Bellingham/Otterburn Group of parishes. Building attributed to Dobson.
Times of Sunday Services:
1st Sunday 11.00 a.m. The Eucharist (BCP)
2nd Sunday 11.00 a.m. The Eucharist (ASB)
3rd Sunday 11.00 a.m. The Eucharist (ASB)
4th Sunday 11.00 a.m. Mattins
                6.00 p.m. The Eucharist (ASB)
Telephone: Vicarage – Otterburn 20212
Road Location: On A696 in the centre of Otterburn Village.

St. Mungo's Church, Simonburn
The mother church of the North Tyne Valley. Its foundation is attributed to the sixth century bishop St. Mungo who was driven from his cell at Glasgow by the pagan King Morken and undertook a missionary journey through Cumbria to North Wales. The original parish extended from Hadrian's Wall to Carter Bar and was at one time the largest parish in England. There are traces of an Anglian church of the ninth century but the present building is mainly thirteenth century with sensitive eighteenth and nineteenth century restorations. There is a particularly fine double piscina still in regular use.
Times of Sunday Services:
See church notice board
Telephone: Rectory – Humshaugh 220 or 304
Road Location: B6320, 4 miles north of Chollerford towards Bellingham.

St. Aidan's Church, Thockrington
Thockrington Church recently attributed to St. Aidan as patron saint was first built in AD 1100 by the Norman family of Umfraville. It remained in their possession with the adjoining lands until 1226 when they were forfeited to the Archbishop of York as compensation for disturbance to the peace of the Prior of Hexham and damage done to the Archbishop's lands by Richard Umfraville. This appropriation is unique in the church history of Northumberland and had to be confirmed by the Bishop of Durham and by papal licence.

The church is built on a spur of the Whin Sill and commands magnificent views. Of the AD 1100 church the chancel walls and other parts remain. Of special interest is the vaulted chancel roof. The grave of Lord Beveridge (National Health Service) is in the churchyard.
Times of Sunday Services:
9.00 a.m. Holy Communion (2nd and 4th Sundays)
Evensongs on special occasions
Telephone: Vicarage – Humshaugh 721
Road Location: From A68 Colwell crossroads go on Rothbury Road and turn off to the left at signpost Thockrington one mile.

St. Aidan's Church, Thorneyburn, Tarset
Consecrated in 1820

Pleasant Georgian church built after the Battle of Trafalgar and the parish created to accommodate redundant fleet chaplains, by Greenwich Hospital, with sister churches in the North Tyne Valley, see Greystead.

Times of Sunday Services:
9.00 a.m. Holy Communion (4th Sunday on month)
3.30 p.m. Evensong (2nd Sunday in month)
Telephone: Bellingham Rectory – Bellingham 20225
Road Location: 1 mile beyond Greenhaugh village, north of Tarset.

St. George's Church, Wall
Consecrated in 1897

Small rectangular church by Hicks and Charlewood. Prior to being built, the parishioners attended services at the parish church of St. Oswald in Lee about 1½ miles away on the B6318.

Times of Sunday Services:
9.00 a.m. Holy Communion with Hymns (ASB)
6.00 p.m. Evensong (BCP)
Telephone: Vicarage – Humshaugh 354
Road Location: A6079 – 4 miles north of Hexham.

St. Mary's Church, Bingfield, Wall

Small rectangular church – present building is mainly late eighteenth century or early nineteenth century. Access to it is by path adjacent to farm buildings of Bingfield Farm.

The church is one of three churches in the parish of St. Oswald in Lee and pre-1879 it was a chapel-of-ease to St. John Lee.

Times of Sunday Services:
10.30 a.m. Holy Communion (1st and 3rd Sundays each month)
Telephone: Vicarage – Humshaugh 354
Road Location: Turning off A68 at the Old Bingfield School on to unclassified road for 1 mile (signposted Bingfield).

St. Oswald in Lee, Heavenfield, Wall

This small rectangular church, rebuilt in 1737 is on the site at Heavenfield where Oswald, King of Northumbria and Martyr defeated Cadwalla in 634 AD, after erecting a wooden cross on the battlefield and commanding his soldiers to pray.

It is the parish church and formed part of the parish of St. John Lee up to the year 1879.

Times of Services:
9.30 a.m. Holy Communion (Easter Sunday)
9.30 a.m. Holy Communion (First Sunday in August –
6.00 p.m. Evensong   Patronal Festival Services)
11.30 p.m. Holy Communion (Christmas Eve)
6.00 p.m. Evensong (First Sunday during summer months)
All services (BCP 1662)
Telephone: Vicarage – Humshaugh 354
Road Location: B6318 – 1 mile from Chollerford.

St. Michael's Church, Wark
Consecrated in 1818

The third church in Wark is a fine example of Regency Gothic. The first church was built in memory of King Aldwarf, murdered in 688, and the second around 1100. There are no remains of these save for a mediaeval font basin. The Admiralty acquired land in North Tyneside after the 1715 Jacobite rising and built the 'Admiralty Churches' of which this is one. The Altar Cross once stood on the altar of the Chapel of Buckingham Palace and had been given to the palace by Tsar Nicholas II. It was given to Wark by King George V.

Times of Sunday Services:
8.15 a.m. Holy Communion (1st Sunday)
10.00 a.m. 2nd Sunday
6.30 p.m. Evening – all Sundays except 2nd (3.00 p.m. winter)
Telephone: Rectory – Bellingham 30223 or Humshaugh 304
Road Location: Out of the village on the road to Bellingham B6320.

All Saints Church, West Woodburn
Consecrated in 1907

Perhaps the chief feature of this fine church is its magnificent setting in the Rede Valley just a few yards from the river. It contains some very fine woodwork, including a splendid carved reredos containing the figures of Saints Cuthbert and Oswald.

Times of Sunday Services:
11.00 a.m. Eucharist
Telephone: Vicarage – West Woodburn 60235
Road Location: 16 miles on A68 from Corbridge.

St. Peter's, Bywell.

CORBRIDGE DEANERY

St. Mary's Church, Blanchland
Consecrated in 1165
Founded as a Premonstratensian Abbey church (the abbey cloister was where the present village stands) the church has pre-Reformation remains such as tombstones, fragments of mediaeval glass etc. It was rebuilt, after depredations by Scots and Henry VIII's men, out of the bequest of Nathaniel Lord Crewe in 1751-52. The nave woodwork is nineteenth century.
Times of Sunday Services:
9.15 a.m. Holy Communion
3.30 p.m. Evensong (summer)
Telephone: Vicarage – Blanchland 207
Road Location: B6306.

St. Andrew's Church, Bywell
Traditionally founded by St. Wilfrid in the seventh century. The outstanding feature is the pre-conquest tower which shows early Saxon work and the Roman material used. The chancel arch and that to the south transept are thirteenth century. Other early features are the 'Lepers Squint' and the piscina in the south transept.

On the outside many early grave slabs have been built into the outer wall of the north transept when it was added in the nineteenth century. These date from before 1295.

Formerly the parish church of Riding Mill and Broomhaugh and known as the 'White Church' it was vested in the Redundant Churches fund on 16 April 1975.
Times of Sunday Services:
One yearly service of Evensong: 1662 order
Telephone: Vicarage Riding Mill 240
Road Location: Bywell near Stocksfield.

St. Peter's Church, Bywell
Date of Consecration Saxon, Monastic

Egbert, consecrated Bishop of Lindisfarne here in AD 803. After Norman Conquest, Patronage given to Benedictines of Durham. Order of secular Canons here in early times. Canons from Durham, living under rule.

Most of the present building is late thirteenth century, and the lancet windows at the east end are superb example of the Early English style. The North Chapel was endowed by the Neville family as a chantry in the fourteenth century, and after the Reformation was used as the village school, separated by a wall from the main building. The church was extensively restored in the mid-nineteenth century.

Times of Sunday Services:
  8.00 a.m. Holy Communion (1662)
11.15 a.m. Mattins (1662)
  6.30 p.m. Evensong (1662)
Services alternating with St. John's, Stocksfield, so Notice Board or Porch Notices must be consulted
Telephone: Vicarage – Stocksfield 2272
Road Location: St. Peter in Bywell. St. John, Meadowfield Road, Stocksfield.

St. Andrew's Church, Corbridge
Consecrated in AD 676

It is reasonably certain that when he built the Abbey Church of Saint Andrew at Hexham, Saint Wilfrid also built Saint Andrew's, Corbridge. Few remains of that earliest church are to be seen now, though there is a Roman arch reminiscent of the Via Dolorosa in Jerusalem which was introduced from the Roman camp by the Saxons to support the arch leading from the porch into the nave. People come from all parts to see it, as they do the original doorway at the west end of the church, which is now filled in by a window and stones.

Times of Sunday Services:
  8.00 and 9.45 a.m. Holy Communion
10.45 a.m. Mattins
  6.00 p.m. Evening Prayer
Telephone: Vicarage – Corbridge 2128
Road Location: Market Place, Corbridge.

St. Mary Magdalene, Dilston Hall

The Chapel of Saint Mary Magdalene is situated in the grounds of Dilston Hall now occupied by the Royal Society for Mentally Handicapped Children. Access is at service times (normally on Saturday morning at 9.30 a.m. and on the 3rd Sunday of each month) or at other times with the consent of the Director of Dilston Hall. It was used by the famous Radcliffe family who were Roman Catholics until after the execution of James, the 3rd Earl of Derwentwater, when it passed into the hands of the Greenwich Hospital Commission and was placed under the pastoral care of the Church of England. Knowledge of this Chapel and its associations has increased by the publication of the popular novel by Anya Seton, 'Devil Water'. Josephine Butler must have worshipped in the Chapel in her formative years.

Times of Sunday Services:
3.00 p.m. Evensong (3rd Sunday in month)
Telephone: Corbridge Vicarage – Corbridge 2128
Road Location: Slaley Road from Corbridge.

St. Oswald, St. Cuthbert and King Alfwald's Church
Halton

On 23 September 788, Alfwald, King of Bernicia (Northumberland) was murdered and his body carried in mournful procession to Hexham Abbey for burial. A light from heaven is said to have shone on the place of his murder, where a church was raised to the honour of St. Oswald, St. Cuthbert and King Alfwald, probably on the site of the present Halton Church.

In 1296 the wooden building was burnt by the Scots, but later rebuilt of stone.

By 1706 this also was in a ruinous condition and although again built up by the then Lord of the Manor (Mr John Douglas), it needed restoration once more in 1880

There are some Roman stones built into the walls of the present church, and the chancel arch is Norman.

Times of Sunday Services:
9.15 a.m. Mattins (2nd Sunday in month)
9.15 a.m. Holy Communion (4th Sunday in month)
9.15 a.m. All festivals
Telephone: Vicarage – Corbridge 2128
Road Location: Halton village, near Corbridge.

St. John's Church, Healey
Consecrated in 1860

St. John's, Healey, originally a Chapel of Ease in the parish of Bywell. Erection of church completed in 1860, architect C. E. Davis of Bath. Original structure was intended to be Norman in style, the roof to be a semi-circular arch all of stone (now of wood). The stone arch was abandoned after two attempts, both of which when the supports were removed fell to the ground! The tower was added in 1890, providing a vestry on the lower part. Note: very unusual Rose window in west wall; three stained glass windows inserted in the Apse in 1883 by Baguley of Newcastle in memory of Robert Ormston of Healey Hall; also, more recently, three windows in memory of members of the Warde-Aldam family also of Healey Hall, scenes taken from the life of St. Cuthbert designed and executed by L. C. Evetts. Well worth a visit.

Times of Sunday Services:
 8.00 a.m. Holy Communion
10.30 a.m. Parish Communion
Telephone: Vicarage – Riding Mill 316
Road Location: Turn 2nd right A68 south from Riding Mill.

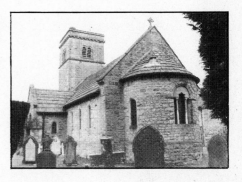

St. Andrew's Church, Heddon on the Wall
Year of consecration Ancient c.680

Ancient hilltop church on pre-conquest foundations. 'Long-and-short' work outside east gable of south aisle; choir (c.680) with preconquest doorheads; Norman sanctuary (c.1170) with zig-zag decoration, vaulted ceiling and roundheaded window; nave (c.1190-1250) with matching western way (1845). Ancient Cross, stone coffin lid, and 'churchwarden's' chest displayed in church. Single bell re-cast 1704; organ 1873. 'Jesse' east window (1873); all other windows since stained depicting 26 saints and others. Churchyard has stones from 1700. Registers from 1656 at County Record Office. Keys at vicarage west of church. Hadrian's Wall visible quarter mile east of church.

Times of Sunday Services:
8.00 a.m. Holy Communion (said)
9.30 a.m. Holy Communion (sung)
6.00 p.m. Evensong (sung)
Telephone: Vicarage – Wylam 3142
Road Location: 8 miles west of Newcastle on B6258 (signed Heddon) off A69. Church opposite Swan Inn in centre of village.

St. James' Church, Hunstanworth
Consecrated in 1863

In the high gothic style of the period this big church was designed by J. H. Teulon, an English architect whose French origins are betrayed by the Burgundian style slate patterning of the roof. The First World War memorial at the west is almost unique and the beautiful little hand blown organ is said to have been in the Great Exhibition of 1851.
Times of Sunday Services:
10.30 a.m. Holy Communion/Mattins
Telephone: Vicarage – Blanchland 207
Road Location: Road south of Blanchland.

Holy Trinity, Matfen
Consecrated in 1842

The church dedicated to the Holy Trinity, is situated on the south side of the Pont, overlooking the Village of Matfen.

It was erected in 1842 at the sole cost of Sir Edward Blackett, and consists of nave, chancel and tower, which houses three bells.

The style of architecture is Early English with single lancet windows.

Matfen was constituted a separate parish in February 1846.

After a period of years the patronage of the living was conveyed by the founder to the Bishop of Newcastle and it has recently been reconveyed to the Crown.

The organ given by Ursula Lady Blackett was built recently by Mr. Nigel Church.
Times of Sunday Services:
10.45 a.m. Holy Communion
Telephone: Vicarage – Stamfordham 456
Road Location: North from Military Road at Matfen Piers.

St. George's Church, Mickley
Consecrated in 1867

The first building on the site of the present church was a 'Chapel of Ease' (1823), as the area was part of the ancient parish of Ovingham. Mickley was given parochial status in 1867 and the 'Chapel' was extended in 1884 by the addition of a chancel, transcepts, and a porch and steeple. The original building became the nave and the church has had no further structural alterations since 1884. Both the building and alterations were paid for by Mr Battie Wrightson the land and coal owner of the period.
Times of Sunday Services:
 8.00 a.m. Holy Communion (said)
10.00 a.m. Parish Communion (sung)
 6.00 p.m. Evensong
Telephone: Vicarage – Stocksfield 3342
Road Location: Side road off A695 at Mickley Square.

St. James' Church, Newton Hall

In 1857 the Chapel of Ease of St. James, Newton Hall, in the parish of Bywell was constructed after the model of the Chapel of St. Bartholomew's Hospital, near Oxford, and enlarged and consecrated in 1873. It is a beautiful example of a traditional church building and is in many ways like a miniature cathedral. The windows are notable and were designed by Messrs Clayton and Bell of London.

The depopulation of the countryside has diminished the population of the parish to about 150 souls. The Hunday Farm Museum, which has attracted a great deal of attention, is situated in the parish.

Times of Sunday Services:
10.00 a.m. School Service
11.00 a.m. Mattins and Holy Communion
Telephone: Corbridge Vicarage – Corbridge 2128
Road Location: Off A69.

St. Mary the Virgin, Ovingham
Consecrated c.1050

The church probably stands on the site of a Christian meeting place marked by a standing cross (fragment beneath pulpit) and was built during the Tynedale Church expansion of the eleventh century. It boasts the tallest Saxon tower in the valley (the windows are noteworthy). The earlier Saxon nave and chancel were replaced during the thirteenth century (by the Umfravilles of Prudhoe Castle, as an act of thanksgiving) by the present early English chancel and transepts. Note the fine lancet windows. The famous wood engraver Thomas Bewick was born in the parish and is buried in the church. Former vicarage is ancient (1378).

Times of Sunday Services:
9.30 a.m. Holy Communion
6.00 p.m. Evening Prayer
Telephone: Vicarage – 0661 32273
Road Location: The church is in the centre of the village. Approach from A69 or from Prudhoe (A695) along unclassified roads.

St. Mary Magdalene, Prudhoe
Dedicated in 1880

Simple church, no aisles, small transcepts. Sanctuary and chancel furnishings in matching light oak. Lych gate is Prudhoe Town War Memorial. Built from local subscription with support from Duke of Northumberland. Seats about 250 people in comfort.

Times of Sunday Services:
8.00 a.m. Holy Communion
9.30 a.m. Parish Communion
6.00 p.m. Evensong
Telephone: Vicarage – Prudhoe 32595
Road Location: In the centre of Prudhoe.

St. James' Church, Riding Mill
Dedicated in 1858

In 1858 St. James' Chapel of Ease was built largely through the effort of the vicar of Bywell St. Andrews, the Rev. J. Jacques. It was acclaimed as a splendid example of Victorian Gothic village church architecture. During the incumbency of the Rev. Canon Slater 1866-1895 the church was enlarged and the sanctuary and organ added. A new vestry appeal was launched by the Rev. Canon Hinkley in 1962 and the new vestries were dedicated by the Lord Bishop of Newcastle on Sunday 8 December 1963. With the relinquishing of Bywell St. Andrew's as the parish church, St. James' Chapel of Ease became the parish church of St. James' Riding Mill in 1975.

Times of Sunday Services:
  8.00 a.m. Holy Communion (1662)
10.00 a.m. The Parish Communion (Rite A)
  6.00 p.m. Evensong (1662) said
Telephone: Vicarage — Riding Mill 240
Road Location: Centre of village.

All Saints Church, Ryal

All Saints Ryal (in former days spelt Ryall) was built in the middle twelfth century. Standing high on a floor of Ingoe stone, it was earlier destroyed by the Scots in 1296. After years of desolation it was restored in 1878 and the main Norman features were preserved, the grandest of these being the bell tower and beautiful arched doorway. Ancient monuments were set into the west wall, thus preserving history. The beautiful bell, which can be heard for miles around was presented by two brothers. In 1879 dedication took place, and today 'All Saints' Ryal, after an inside restoration in 1971 still functions fortnightly.

Times of Sunday Services:
8.00 a.m. Holy Communion (2nd Sunday of month)
6.00 p.m. Evensong (4th Sunday of month)
3.00 p.m. Winter months (2nd and 4th Sundays)
Telephone: Vicarage — Stamfordham 456
Road Location: 2¾ miles north-west of Matfen on the Matfen to Ingoe road.

St. John's Church, Shotley Low Quarter
Consecrated in 1836

Church built to replace the old parish church of St. Andrew, Kiln Pit Hill. It is situated in the middle of a wide and sparsely populated parish. The style is Early Perpendicular and consists of a chancel, nave, south porch and campanile tower with two bells.

Times of Sunday Services:
10.30 a.m. Holy Communion
Telephone: Vicarage — Edmundbyers 55665
Road Location: On B.6278 from Shotley Bridge to the A68.

St. Andrew's Church, Grey Mare Hill, Shotley
Rebuilt in 1769

Built by Humphrey Hopper of Blackhedley in memory of his wife who died in 1752. The vicarage was at Unthank and is now two houses.

Interesting head stone of Blacksmith John Hunter of Black Hedley died 1796. All the blacksmiths tools are shown on the headstone, the epitaph of which is well worth reading, this church is now not normally used for worship.

Road Location: Kiln Pit Hill, just of A68.

St. Mary the Virgin, Slaley
Thirteenth century church rebuilt in 1832

A place of worship has been in the village of Slaley since AD 1240. Present church was built in 1832, funds for which were raised by the parishioners. It contained a three decker pulpit and had a gallery over the north side of the nave. It was lit by paraffin lamps and had a chimney built on the east end gable (photo in vestry) in 1907 and was further restored and embellished with most of its present furnishings. The Lych Gate was erected in 1921, a memorial to the fallen in the First World War,

Times of Sunday Services:
Alternate Sundays 10.30 a.m. Parish Communion
                8.30 a.m. Holy Communion
            10.30 a.m. Mattins
Telephone: Vicarage – Slaley 212
Road Location: Main road through village.

St. Mary the Virgin, Stamfordham

St. Mary the Virgin was first recorded as being built in 1220, then rebuilt in 1848 in the time of the Rev. Bigg. Many of the original stones and arches were cleaned and reused. Some of the grave crosses are inserted in the porch walls. Two of the pillars have ornamental caps, perhaps imitations of the ones at the entrance to Solomon's temple. The banner now hanging in the north aisle used to hang over Lord Stamfordham's stall in Westminster Abbey. On the chancel floor lies the sandstone body of a legless knight supposed to be Sir John De Felton who was Lord of the Matfen manor (also Sheriff of Northumberland) in 1390. At the west end of the church is a large altar shaped stone in memory of John Swinburn and his wife Marie bearing the inscription 'A loving wife and mother dear, such a one who now lieth here. 1623'.

Times of Sunday Services:
9.15 a.m. Holy Communion
Teleohone: Vicarage – Stamfordham 456
Road Location: B6309.

41

St. John the Divine, Stocksfield
Consecrated in 1927

Built as a Chapel-of-Ease to cater for the rapidly growing centre of population in the Stocksfield area of the parish: west end designed to allow for extension. Furnishings in memory of former parishioners or provided by public subscription.

Times of Sunday Services:
9.30 a.m. Parish Communion (Rite A. ASB)
6.30 p.m. Evensong (1662)
Services alternating with St. Peter's, so Notice Board or Porch Notices must be consulted
Telephone: Vicarage – Stocksfield 2272
Road Location: Meadowfield Road, Stocksfield.

St. Philip and St. James, Whittonstall
Consecrated in 1830

Pevsner describes the building of 1830 (Architect Jonathon Marshall) as having straight-headed mullioned windows under hood-moulds on the south wall and a small embattled west tower. (The north wall has no windows.) The chancel was added in 1896 and is higher and more ambitious than the nave. A fragment of an Early English capital is displayed in the porch, which, together with some old tomb slabs, are the only remnants of an earlier building on this site.

Times of Sunday Services:
9.00 a.m. Holy Communion (3rd Sunday in month only)
6.00 p.m. Evensong (1st Sunday in month only)
Telephone: Vicarage – Edmundbyers 55665 (STD 0207)
Road Location: On west side of B6309 between Ebchester and Stocksfield.

St. Oswin's Church, Wylam

Wylam St. Oswin was built through the generosity of George Hedley, son of the famous railway pioneer of Wylam, William Hedley. It was dedicated on All Saints Day, 1886. Designed by the Newcastle architect R. J. Johnson, the church is in the perpendicular style, aisleless and with a large tower on the south side. St. Oswin, king and martyr, is depicted in a stained window on the south side of the chancel. This is the only church in the diocese dedicated to the Northumbrian saint. The village of Wylam remained within the parish of Ovingham until 1902, when the separate parish of Wylam with Horsley was established.

Times of Sunday Services:
8.00 a.m. Holy Communion
9.00 a.m. Mattins
9.45 a.m. Parish Communion
6.30 p.m. Evensong
Telephone: Vicarage – Wylam 3254
Road Location: West of Newcastle; south off A69.

Holy Cross Church, Haltwhistle.

ᴴEXHAM ᴰEANERY

St. Cuthbert's Church, Allendale
Consecrated in 1873

There has been a church in Allendale from early times. The Chapel of Our Lady of Allendale was vested in the Prior of Hexham in 1174 by an Agreement between the Bishop of Durham and the Archbishop of York. It is further mentioned by Archbishop Romayne of York in 1294. A new church was built in the fourteenth century. In 1807 that church was replaced by an excessively plain building; fortunately demolished in 1873, and replaced by the present church. The most striking interior feature of this church is the beautiful reredos in alabaster and mosiac depicting the Last Supper. For reasons unknown the dedication of the church was changed after many centuries to that of 'St. Cuthbert'.

Times of Sunday Services:
8.00 a.m. Holy Eucharist
11.00 a.m. Sung Eucharist
6.00 p.m. Evensong
Telephone: Vicarage – Allendale 983 336
Road Location: From Hexham: B6305, B6304, B6303.

St. Augustine's Church, Alston
Consecrated in 1870

First record of a church in Alston between the years 1154-1189. The present church was built in 1869, the former being pulled down. The church spire was erected in 1886. Note the beautiful reredos depicting 'The Adoration of the Lamb'. In 1767 the Greenwich Hospital gave to the church the Derwent Water Bell and Clock belonging to the Earl of the same name. In 1978 the clock was restored and put in the church as a working exhibit. There are ten bells in the tower, one of which is the Derwent Water Bell recast. They can all be played by one man as the ropes are attached to a keyboard. The dedication is to St. Augustine of Canterbury.

Times of Sunday Services:
10.30 a.m. Holy Communion
10.30 a.m. Holy Communion (Wednesdays)
Telephone: Vicarage – Alston 81317
Road Location: Front Street, Alston.

45

St. Cuthbert's Church, Beltingham

Perpendicular, oldest parts fifteenth century, masons marks in windows. Stained glass in memory of members of Lowes family and Douglas Smiths and in thanksgiving for safety of members of Bowes-Lyon family in 1904 accident. Tablet in memory of Rev. Anthony Hedley of Vindolanda fame (died 1856). Bishop Nicholas Ridley possibly baptised in the church. Organ, one-manual Harrison.

Times of Sunday Services:
  8.15 a.m. Holy Communion (fortnightly)
10.45 a.m. Holy Communion (monthly)
10.45 a.m. Mattins (monthly)
  6.30 p.m. Evensong (fortnightly).
Telephone: Vicarage – Bardon Mill 331
Road Location: South of A69, Bardon Mill.

St. Paul's Church, Catton
Dedicated in 1900s

The church was built during the incumbency of the Rev'd. H. S. Stephenson, Rector of Allendale 1900-1908, as a daughter church to St. Cuthbert's, Allendale. It is a simple 'mission type' building with no outstanding architectural merit.

Times of Sunday Services:
9.45 a.m. Holy Eucharist on second and fourth Sundays in the month
Telephone: Vicarage – Allendale 983 336
Road Location: From Hexham: B6305, B6304.

St. Aidan's Church, Fourstones
Dedicated in 1892

Built by the Incumbent, the Rev. George Cruddas at his own expense, as a mission church. Still referred to locally as 'The Mission' as well as St. Aidans. Small wooden church on stone foundation, slate roof.

Times of Sunday Services:
9.45 a.m. Holy Communion
3.00 p.m. Evensong (5th Sunday in month)
Telephone: Vicarage – Hexham 603910
Road Location: Main road opposite Fourstones Post Office.

St. John's Church, Garrigill, Alston, Cumbria
Advowson granted to Canons of Hexham Abbey 1215
Present building 1790
Pewter chalic (Queen Anne). Register of non-conformists of early years kept in church.
War Memorial 1939-1945 painted by local lady.
Christianity in Garrigill region in Anglo-Saxon days and fully established in early Norman records. (See 'Capella de Guardegile' by Ceasar Carne).
Times of Sunday Services:
11.15 a.m. Holy Communion (1st Sunday in month)
5.00 p.m. Evensong on other Sundays
Telephone: Vicarage — Alston 81317
Road Location: Off A689 Alston-Middleton in Teasdale road.

St. Cuthbert's Church, Greenhead
The Lord of the Manor of Blenkinsopp gave land on which a chapel was built in 1828. This was within the parish of Haltwhistle but served the local population, rapidly increasing, to work in the Blenkinsopp colliery, and on the construction of the Newcastle-Carlisle railway. The chapel was designed by the architect Mr. Dobson. In 1900 Col Joicey arranged for a chancel to be built in memory of his father and at this time the nave was restored and a spire added to the tower. The oak reredos, pannelling, pulpit and choir stalls are characteristic of this period. The east window represents Christ in Majesty, King Oswald and his Queen, and some well known Northumbrian Saints of the sixth and seventh centuries.
Times of Sunday Services:
11.00 a.m. HC or MP (alternately)
Road Location: A69.

St. Cuthbert's Church,
Greenhead.

Holy Cross Church, Haltwhistle
Parish Church of Haltwhistle — important town in the Middle Ages — built on site probably connected with Saint Aidan and Saint Paulinus. An original example of thirteenth century architecture; built in one style and in one period. Restored 1870. Nave and aisles wide in proportion to length and appear to form a square. Chancel is disproportionately long in comparison with the nave. East window has thirteenth century triplet of lancets and excellent glass by William Morris. Local features include Ridley Memorial Stone, Grave effigies with Blenkinsopp and Thirlwell connections and a seventh century water stoup which may have been used by Paulinus.
Times of Sunday Services:
8.00 a.m. Holy Communion (said)
9.30 a.m. Holy Communion (sung)
6.30 p.m. Evening Prayer
Telephone: Vicarage — 0498 20215
Road Location: Off A69 sixteen miles west of Hexham.

47

St. Cuthbert's Church, Haydon Bridge
Consecrated in 1796

Parish church is built upon land donated by Greenwich Hospital and the chancel was extended in 1890s. The nave windows and two on south side of chancel gothicised. 'Pagoda' type roof on tower unusual and a feature of the furnishings is an alabaster and marble font. Four of the stained glass windows are by Kempe (c.1900).

Times of Sunday Services:
1st and 3rd: 10.00 a.m. Parish Communion
     6.00 p.m. Evensong
2, 4, 5th 8.00 a.m. Holy Communion
    10.00 a.m. Mattins
     6.00 p.m. Evensong
Telephone: Vicarage – Haydon Bridge 307
Road Location: A69 to Haydon Bridge turn right from east, turn left from west into Church Street.

Haydon Old Church

An interesting building for the ecclesiologist with a possible early date of 1190 for the original structure. The evidence is the east end which has three stepped round headed lancet windows and the chancel of the original church, with a chantry added in the fourteenth century. A chapel in a south aisle, is all that remains, and the west end is part of a restoration by C. C. Hodges in 1882. The font is a Roman altar, probably obtained from a site on or near the Roman Wall.

The key for the old church can be obtained from Haydon Bridge Vicarage.
Location: ½ mile north of Haydon Bridge, up the hill.

All Hallows' Church, Henshaw
Dedicated: Laying of foundation stone – 29 June 1888

East window, St. Hilda by Ruth and Holman Hunt, 'Light of the World'. Put in by Armstrongs of Hardriding. South window in memory of Mr. Ingledew, Secretary and Registrar to the 1st Bishop of Newcastle.

Times of Sunday Services:
8.15 a.m. Holy Communion (fortnightly)
9.15 a.m. Holy Communion (fortnightly)
6.30 p.m. Evensong (fortnightly)
Telephone: Vicarage – Bardon Mill 331
Road Location: Old A69 west of Bardon Mill.

The Priory and Parish Church of St. Andrew, Hexham
Consecrated in AD 674

The Saxon Abbey was founded in AD 674 by St. Wilfrid, who later became Bishop of Hexham. In 875 the Danes raided Hexham and both church and town were destroyed; the crypt, the eastern apse, the font, the 'frith' or 'peace' stool and a small chalice survived from that period.

In 1113, Archbishop Thomas of York handed it over to the Augustinian Canons. They established it as one of their Priories, repaired and extended the building (the present transepts and choir are their work). There are many treasures of this period in the church — windows, columns and arches, the 'Night Stairs', the magnificent late fifteenth century wooden screen separating the 'Crossing' from the choir, the misericordia seats in the choir, the beautiful 'Triptych' in the Ogle chantry, more than 100 mediaeval paintings on wooden panels and, in stone, the 'Tree of Life', and the more humourous figures round the Leschman Chantry. In 1297, a final devastating Scottish raid destroyed the nave, and, until modern times, the church remained with only the transepts and choir in use.

A Rector of Hexham, Canon Savage, succeeded in 1908 in having the nave rebuilt to the designs of Mr. Temple Moore.
Times of Sunday Services:
8.30 a.m. Holy Communion (series 2, said)
10.00 a.m. Family Communion and Children's Church (Rite A, sung)
11.15 a.m. Mattins (1st Sunday — Holy Communion BCP)
6.30 p.m. Choral Evensong (full choir)
Telephone: Rectory — Hexham 602031
Verger — Hexham 602737
Road Location: Off Market Place, Hexham. A69 Newcastle to Carlisle.

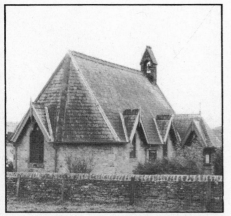

St. Mary's Church, Lowgate, Hexham
Consecrated in 1894
The church was built by Mr. J. Saint in 1894 at a cost of £426 on ground given by Mr. Lumley of Blossom Hill. The initiative for the building was taken by Canon Barker, Rector of Hexham Abbey since 1866, who had been taking services in Bagraw schoolroom, now the WI hut. The east window, an adaption of Holman Hunt's 'Light of the World' was made by the Gateshead Glass Company and given by Mr. W. Briddick. The porch was added by Mr. and Mrs. J. C. Straker in memory of their infant son. The dedication to St. Mary was appropriate because St. Mary's Church on the south side of Hexham Market Place had also been a chapel-of-ease to the Abbey.
Times of Sunday Services:
10.00 a.m. HC 2nd and 4th Sundays
11.00 a.m. Sunday School (not 4th Sunday)
Telephone: Hexham Rectory — Hexham 602031
Road Location: Allendale Rd., B6305 from Hexham.

Holy Paraclete Church, Kirkhaugh
Dedicated in 1869 (replacing a mediaeval church)

The only church in England which bears the dedication 'Paraclete'. There is no village in the parish, only a widespread collection of farms and homesteads and it is in Northumberland although it forms part of the benefice of Alston Moor churches in Cumbria. Its population is 45. The Parish history is recorded since the late twelfth century. The church has no pews, only chairs. The ancient chalice is dated 1571. Saxon Cross in churchyard.
Times of Sunday Services:
Holy Communion or Evening Prayer
1st, 3rd and 5th Sundays at 6.30 p.m. March-Oct.
3 p.m. November-February.
Telephone: Alston Vicarage 81317
Road Location: Branch road off Alston/Hexham A686 road, ¼ mile from town. Approximately 2 miles from Alston to Kirkhaugh.

St. Jude's Church, Knaresdale
Dedicated in 1838

First mention of the church is dated 1680 in connection with repairs to the building and the bell. It was rebuilt in 1838. The churchyard has a strange epitaph to Robert Baxter who died in 1796.
Times of Sunday Services:
3.00 p.m. HC and EP (2nd and 4th Sundays)
Telephone: Alston Vicarage – Alston 317
Road Location: On the A689 to Alston.

Saint Mary and Saint Patrick's Church
Lambley

Near the river is the site of a small convent of Benedictine Nuns which was destroyed in 1296 by the Scots. It was restored but later dissolved by Henry VIII when it had six inmates and a revenue of £5.15s 8d a year. The present church dated 1885 by William Searle Hicks.
Times of Sunday Services:
10.30 a.m. Holy Communion
Telephone: Haltwhistle 20430
Road Location: B6292, Brampton to Alston road.

St. John's Church, Nenthead
Consecrated on 14 August 1845

Pulpit and reading desk are partly ancient. The altar is a refectory table several centuries old, the communion rail is mediaeval. The kneeling runner is handmade. The altar cross was made by a local craftsman.

The church was built in four months, the previous attempt having collapsed. Geographically the church is considered the highest in England, Nenthead being the highest village.

Times of Sunday Services:
11.15 a.m. Holy Communion or Mattins
Telephone: Alston Vicarage 81317
Road Location: Via Vicarage Terrace turn between Chapel and Reading Room.

St. Peter's Church, Newbrough
Consecrated in 1170

Built on site of fourth century Roman Mile castle. First church built in twelfth century. Present building erected in 1866. Chapel of ease for Newbrough in Warden Parish.

Times of Sunday Services:
Summer and Festivals only
10.45 a.m. Holy Communion
 6.30 p.m. Evensong
Telephone: Vicarage – Hexham 603910
Road Location: Main road $\frac{1}{4}$ mile beyond Newbrough Town Hall in Carlisle direction.

St. Mark's Church, Ninebanks
Dedicated in 1871

Originally a chapel of ease in the Parish of Allendale, a church was built in 1764 and consecrated by the Archbishop of York. It was made a separate parish in 1767. The church was rebuilt in 1813 and again in 1871. A small building in the early English style with a nave and chancel. The first Vicar was appointed in 1867 when he was also given charge of the Church of Carrshield. United in 1953 with Whitfield, retaining independent Parish status. Then in 1979 the joint Parishes were joined with the United Parish of Allendale to form the new Benefice of Allendale with Whitfield.

Times of Sunday Services:
10.00 a.m. Sung Eucharist on the first Sunday in the month
Telephone: Vicarage – Allendale 983 336
Road Location: A686 or from Allendale Town Square.

St. John of Beverley Church
Consecrated in 1843
St. John Lee

A church has stood on or near this spot ever since the seventh century, when (as Bede tells us), St. John of Beverley, while still a Monk at Hexham Abbey, came here frequently to pray, and on one occasion healed a dumb boy.

The present building dates from 1843 and is basically the work of John Dobson of Newcastle, but was extended and much beautified by W. S. Hicks in 1886. Notable features: the wooden ceiling and chancel-screen; mediaeval stone carvings from a former church on this site; a Roman altar, later used as a Christian font; some pleasant nineteenth and twentieth century windows; and the 'Oakwood Stone' with cup and ring markings possibly 6000 years old.

Times of Sunday Services:
9.30 a.m. Holy Communion
6.30 p.m. Evensong
Telephone: Rectory – Hexham 602220
Road Location: Well sign-posted from large round-about on A69 outside Hexham.

St. Aidan's Church, Stagshaw House, Nr. Corbridge
Consecrated in 1885

This is a private chapel situated in the grounds of Stagshaw House and owned by Mrs. J. J. Straker, though the services are open to the public. Built in Gothic style, the church is small but well-appointed; pulpit, lectern and reredos display good craftsmanship in wood; there is an elegant spire and (when the weather is fine) a beautiful view across the Tyne valley.

Times of Sunday Services:
11.15 a.m. Mattins (Holy Communion 1st Sunday of each month and on greater festivals)
Telephone: St. John Lee Rectory – Hexham 602220
Road Location: Sandhoe Road, off A68 approximately 2 miles north of Corbridge.

St. Michael and All Angels, Warden
Consecrated in AD 704

Warden church founded by St. Wilfrid in AD 704. The church was rebuilt in 1764-5 by the exertions of Sir Walter Blackett of Wallington. The eleventh century arch connecting the nave with the base of the tower is the oldest part of the building and many of the stones forming this arch are Roman. Note also: Saxon grave cover in chancel on north side in front of altar rail, also grave cover on south side. Chancel owes its present appearance to Rev. George Cruddas, vicar 1867-95 and reflects revived interest in mediaeval architecture. Church tower with four successive stages, bottom stage probably being the oldest Saxon tower in Northumberland.

Times of Sunday Services:
8.00 a.m. Holy Communion (1st, 3rd and 5th Sundays)
11.00 a.m. Holy Communion (2nd Sunday)
11.00 a.m. Mattins (4th Sunday)
6.30 p.m. Evening Prayer (3rd Sunday)
Times modified in winter – check locally
Telephone: Vicarage – Hexham 603910
Road Location: 300 yards from Warden Bridge over South Tyne at confluence of North and South Tyne.

St. John's Church, Whitfield
Dedicated in 1813

The present building consisting of chancel and one bay of nave is all that remains of the old parish church built in 1813. The stones of the remainder of the church and tower were used in the construction of the new church. The registers date from 1612. It is uncertain whether St. John's stands on the site of the original church. The list of Rectors begins in 1180 with Robert de Quitfield, which confirms the existence of a church at that time. The Whitfields ruled the area for over 600 years; yet there is neither monument or any relic of that family in the church. What remains of the building is good.

Times of Sunday Servcies:
The church is used during the winter for economical reasons instead of the parish church.
Telephone: Vicarage – Allendale 983 336
Road Location: Whitfield Village then Haltwhistle Road.

The Holy Trinity, Whitfield
Dedicated in 1860

The 'New' Parish Church was the gift of the Rev'd. and Mrs. J. A. Blackett-Ord in memory of William Ord Esq., from whom Mrs. Blackett-Ord had inherited his whole estate. A very beautiful church in early English style. The church abounds in craftsmanship in stone, wood, wrought-iron and glass. It contains many memorials to the Blackett-Ord family; dedicated patrons and generous benefactors to the church and community from the time of their ownership of Whitfield to the present. A beautiful church in a glorious setting: well-worth a visit.

Times of Sunday Services:
10.00 a.m. Sung Eucharist (except on first Sunday in month)
Evening Services as announced
Telephone: Vicarage – Allendale 983 336
Road Location: From Hexham B6035, B6295, A686.

St. Helen's Church, Whitley Chapel
Consecrated in 1764

The church building is of uncertain date. Prior to 1764, it was a Chapel of ease served by Hexham Abbey, but in that year it became the Parish Church of the district known as Hexhamshire, lying between Hexham and Blanchland. It is thought to have been consecrated in 1764 by the Archbishop of York. The church is a simple building of stone, without aisles, with a later vestry built on to the west end. Fixed to the walls of the nave are four wooden panels, dated 1858, inscribed with the Ten Commandments, Apostles' Creed and Lord's Prayer. The panelling on either side of the altar is in memory of the Revd. William Sisson, Vicar of the Parish from 1841 to 1906.

Times of Sunday Services:
9.30 a.m. Every Sunday – Holy Communion with hymns and sermon
Telephone: Vicarage – Slaley 379
Road Location: Hamlet of Whitley Chapel, Hexhamshire off B6306.

Jesmond Parish Church.

NEWCASTLE CENTRAL DEANERY

Saint Cuthbert's Church, Brunswick Village

The foundation stone was laid in 1905 when the Reverend W. A. King was Vicar of Dinnington, which included this village. Built of colliery bricks and red facing bricks. A grant from the Carnegie Trust helped to pay for the organ by Harrison & Harrison of Durham but a second keyboard was never completed.

Times of Services: See Notice Board
Telephone: Vicarage – Ponteland 71377
Road Location: Left hand side of main road to Dinnington.

St. Matthew's Church, Dinnington
Dedicated in 1886

Captain Henry Bell, of Woolsington had the church built at a cost of £3000. It is built of stone and is in the transition period between Early English and decorated styles. It consists of a chancel, nave, south porch and a western turret containing one bell. The reredos was given to the church in 1959. It was originally given to the first Bishop of Newcastle in 1882 by the women of the diocese, for the Bishops Chapel at Benwell Towers. Seating capacity 200. Tablets on the walls are memorials to the family of Henry Bell and the 'Village dead' of two World Wars.

Times of Sunday Services:
9.30 a.m. Family Communion
6.00 p.m. Evensong
Telephone: Vicarage – Ponteland 71377
Road Location: Main Street, Dinnington.

All Saints' Church, Gosforth
Consecrated in 1887

All Saints', Gosforth, is a fine example of Gothic Revival architecture and its interior contains some excellent Victorian wood carving. The Saints are the theme of its stained glass windows which date from 1887 to 1981. The well-proportioned tower of the church is visible on all sides; it houses ten bells and is surmounted by a battlement and flagstaff. Originally the church served a large area which extended towards Dinnington, Ponteland, Whorlton and Sugley. However in recent years new parishes have been created at Cowgate, Kenton, and in the Fawdon area, leaving All Saints responsible for much of the central area of Gosforth and for Kenton Park.

Times for Sunday Services:
7.30 a.m. Mattins
8.00 a.m. Holy Communion
9.15 a.m. Parish Communion
11.30 a.m. Holy Communion
6.30 p.m. Evensong
Telephone: Vicarage – Gosforth 856345
Church Office – Gosforth 857864
Road Location: West Avenue, Gosforth.

St. Nicholas' Church, Gosforth
Consecrated in 1799

The parish is believed to date from Saxon times. It is thought that the church demolished in 1799 replaced the church of those days.

The tower and west end of the present church was erected in 1799. The architect was John Dodds. The enlargement in 1820 on the same Georgian classical lines was the work of John Dobson. Further enlargements were made in 1912/13 and in 1959. Throughout the Middle Ages, the area served by the church was North and South Gosforth, Fawdon, Kenton and Coxlodge. In 1805 the Register shows the marriage of Edward Barrett to Mary Graham Clarke – their daughter Elizabeth married the poet Robert Browning.

Times of Sunday Services:
8.00 a.m. Holy Communion
9.15 a.m. Family Communion
11.00 a.m. Mattins
12 noon Holy Communion (1st and 3rd Sundays and Festival)
6.30 p.m. Evensong
Telephone: Vicarage – Gosforth 851326
Road Location: Church Road, Gosforth.

The Church of the Ascension, Kenton
Consecrated on 14 April 1956

Begun in 1954, The Church of the Ascension was completed in two years and consecrated on 14 April 1956 by Bishop Noel Hudson. It was built to serve the needs of the ever growing North Kenton and Montagu Estates which now have a population of over 20,000.

The church, which is on the site of the old Kenton Quarry, was designed by Newcombe and Newcombe Architects, and built by Messrs J. and W. Lowry. The building is of simple modern design with a pre-stressed concrete roof spanning the whole.

Times of Sunday Services:
8.00 a.m. Holy Communion
9.30 a.m. Sung Eucharist
6.30 p.m. Evensong
Telephone: Vicarage – Newcastle 857803
Road Location: Creighton Avenue, Kenton.

St. Mary the Virgin, Fawdon
Consecrated in 1959

St. Mary's was built as a daughter church of All Saint's, Gosforth, in 1959, and became part of the Team Parish of the Epiphany in 1980. Alterations and extensions in 1979 allowed it to fulfil its planned role as a dual-purpose church/hall to maximum effect. Visitors will come to St. Mary's for the warmth and friendship of the worship rather than for any architectural splendour. Those interested in church embroidery will wish to see a cope, made by one of the congregation, which has been shown at several exhibitions of ecclesiastical embroidery.

Times of Sunday Services:
9.30 a.m. Parish Communion
Telephone: Vicarage — 855403
Road Location: Off Fawdon Lane, 100 yards north of Fawdon metro station, Mapledene Road.

St. Hugh's Church, Gosforth
Consecrated in 1961

St. Hugh's was built in 1960 to serve the Regent Farm, Grange and Grange Park estates within the parish of All Saints, Gosforth, and soon had its own resident curate-in-charge. In 1980 it became one of three churches to form the new parish of The Epiphany, Newcastle, and within the parish was given responsibility for Grange Park, Grange and Regent Farm estates, Coxlodge and St. Nicholas Hospital (where the Team Vicar is chaplain). In 1981 the building was extended to provide additional halls. The church seeks to serve the community and witness to the transcendent presence of Christ.

Times of Sunday Services:
8.00 a.m. Holy Communion (1st Sunday of month)
9.30 a.m. Family Service (1st Sunday of month)
9.30 a.m. Parish Eucharist (Other Sundays)
9.00 p.m. Evening Worship
Telephone: Vicarage — Newcastle 858792
Road Location: Beside Wansbeck Road Metro Station, Gosforth.

Kingston Park — The Epiphany
House Church 1978

The meeting room in the vicarage extension was used for three years as the place of Sunday worship, with creche and children's work in the living and dining rooms. The meeting room is still used for regular services and meetings, in conjunction with the local community hall.

Times of Sunday Services:
8.30 a.m. Holy Communion (Meeting room 2nd and 4th Sundays)
10.00 a.m. Morning Service (Community Hall, 1st Sunday Family Communion)
Telephone: 864050
Road Location: 12 Shannon Court, Kingston Park.

St. Aidan's Church, Brunton Park
Dedicated on 4 May 1956; Consecrated on 4 May 1963

Services were first held in the Northern Rugby Club pavilion in 1944. A Nissen hut was acquired and adapted for use as the first church, being dedicated on 4 May 1946. The present church, originally a multi-purpose building with a stage at the west end and a screen to close the choir during the week was completed ten years later. The architect was a church member, Mr. Fred Herron. When St. Aidan's community centre was built the stage area was altered for use as a baptistry before the church was consecrated in 1963.

Times of Sunday Services:
  7.45 a.m. Holy Communion
  9.30 a.m. Family Communion
11.00 a.m. Family Service (occasional)
  6.30 p.m. Evensong
Telephone: Parsonage – Wideopen 363358
Road Location: At the head of Polwarth Drive, the main road leading into Brunton Park from the Great North Road.

St. Chad's Church, Woodlands Park
Dedicated in 1959

A small dual purpose building erected to serve the 'Woodlands Park' complex of housing estates in the centre of the parish of North Gosforth. A new church designed by C. Soloman Associates will replace St. Chad's and the redundant St. Columba's at Wideopen, and will be shared with the local Methodist congregation.

Times of Sunday Services:
9.30 a.m. Family Communion and Sunday School
Telephone: Vicarage – Newcastle 362280
Road Location: Corner Elmwood Avenue and Pinewood Avenue.

St. Nicholas Cathedral

The Cathedral is for the most part a fourteenth century building surmounted by its famous fifteenth century lantern spire. Much of the interior furnishing dates back to the time of the creation of the new Diocese in 1882. There is one mediaeval window, a rare pre-reformation lectern and a fifteenth century font, two good Renaissance memorials, many interesting wall tablets and some good modern glass. The church replaced earlier buildings the earliest known of which was Norman.

Times of Sunday Services:
8.00 a.m. Holy Communion
9.00 a.m. Mattins
9.30 a.m. Sung Eucharist
6.00 p.m. Evensong
Telephone: Vicarage – Newcastle 853472
          Office – Newcastle 321939
Road Location: $\frac{1}{4}$ mile west of Pilgrim Street Roundabout.

St. Andrew's Church, Newgate Street
Consecration probably 10th century

The building began in the twelfth century was different both in shape and height from the present. The outstanding feature of the original building is the chancel arch with its chevron ornamentation considered one of the finest in the Diocese. The last addition was the south porch in 1726, other additions were the Trinity Chapel, the widened aisles and lengthened chancel and the addition of both transepts. Notable features: the Lepers Squint, the choir stalls of Austrian Oak, the Giordano painting and the mediaeval font cover, considered by some to be one of the finest in England.

Times of Sunday Services:
10.15 a.m. Sung Eucharist
 3.00 p.m. Evensong (Choral last Sunday)
Telephone: Vicarage – 0632 845495
             Church Office – 0632 326090

St. Ann's Church, City Road
Consecrated in 1768

There has been a church on this site since mediaeval times. After the Reformation the church was built and consecrated in 1768. The present church was largely built with stone taken from the City Wall. The church yard is among the last within the city to be closed for burials and is the resting place of many who died in the last great cholera epidemic.

Times of Sunday Services:
9.30 a.m. Parish Mass
6.00 p.m. Evening Prayer
Telephone: Vicarage – Newcastle 320516
Road Location: On the City Road, 150 yards east of Tyne Tees TV Studios.

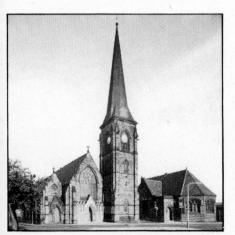

Christ Church, Shieldfield
Consecrated in 1861

This is one of the very best examples of Victorian Gothic buildings – far surpassing many more famous places. It has been sensitively re-ordered to facilitate the modern catholic liturgical reforms but retains a sense of the numinous for which the passer-by seems grateful since the church is open during the day-light hours and is not infrequently used by the casual visitor as a place of quiet prayer in a busy city.

Times of Sunday Services:
 8.00 a.m. Low Mass
10.00 a.m. Parish Mass
 6.30 p.m. Evensong and Benediction
Telephone: Vicarage – Newcastle 320516
Road Location: Almost a city centre church – just east of the central motorway (A6127) from which it can be seen.

St. John the Baptist, Grainger Street
Date of Consecration approx 1145-1245

Items of interest: The fifteenth century font cover and the Jacobean pulpit are fine examples of local woodwork. When the church was restored a new sanctuary was created at the Crossing, which contains a stone altar slab given in 1712 as a reminder of the Church Revival under Queen Anne. For many years the High Altar, it is now the Credence Table. The chancel, now the Lady Chapel contains a window including fragments of mediaeval glass with the earliest known representation of the arms of Newcastle. Further along the wall can be seen a cruciform opening which enabled the anchorite, whose cell was above the present sacristy, to see the altar. The rood and reredos are both the work of Sir Charles Nicholson.

Times of Sunday Services:
- 8.45 a.m. Mattins and Litany
- 9.30 a.m. Parish Communion
- 11.00 a.m. High Mass
- 6.30 p.m. Evensong
- 7.45 p.m. Holy Communion

Weekdays: Daily celebrations*Telephone:* Office — Newcastle 320483

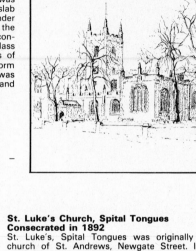

St. Luke's Church, Spital Tongues
Consecrated in 1892

St. Luke's, Spital Tongues was originally a daughter church of St. Andrews, Newgate Street. It became a separate parish in 1892 when the present church was consecrated. It replaced our old corrugated iron mission church and is an imposing building designed by the Newcastle architect H. W. Wood, and built in brick of a pleasing dark red shade and looks out over the town moor. The parish of Spital Tongues which it serves, is now very tiny, but still manages to preserve something of the old atmosphere of the village community it once was, though now well within the boundaries of the city of Newcastle.

Times of Sunday Services:
9.30 a.m. Parish Communion
6.30 p.m. Evensong (said)
Telephone: Vicarage — 323341
Road Location: Claremont Road, Newcastle upon Tyne.

Church of St. Thomas the Martyr, Barras Bridge
Consecrated in 1830

This 'Peculiar' in the City Centre, architect John Dobson, was built by the Trustees of Saint Mary Magdalene and Holy Jesus Hospitals to replace a mediaeval chapel by the Tyne. Until recently the 'Master' was Chaplain to these hospitals: now he is Anglican Chaplain to the University. The fine organ is used for recitals by internationally famous organists.

On weekdays it provides a meeting-place for people of many differing cultures and backgrounds for lunch-time services and private prayer; at the West End a wide variety of literature and special exhibitions; every Wednesday a 'Just Lunch' for discussions of international concern.

Times of Sunday Services:
10.00 a.m. Community Eucharist
6.30 p.m. Choral Evensong (in term-time)
Telephone: University Chaplaincy — 328511 ext 2344
Road Location: Barras Bridge.

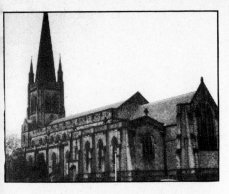

Holy Trinity Church, Jesmond
Consecrated on 24 September 1922

Built as a War Memorial Church commemorating those who gave their lives in the 1914-18 war. The small chapel was already built and used for worship before being added to in 1922. The main areas of interest in the building are the memorial window, made as one set, each in memory of a different regiment and covering all the Services. The organ is a fine example of Messrs Rushworth and Dreapers work. Originally a daughter church of Clayton Memorial Church, it became a Parish Church in 1926.

Times of Sunday Services:
8.30 a.m. Holy Communion (1st and 3rd Sundays)
10.45 a.m. Morning Prayer (Holy Communion 2nd Sunday; Family Service 3rd Sunday)
6.30 p.m. Evening Prayer (Holy Communion 4th Sunday)
Telephone: Vicarage – Newcastle 811663
Road Location: At Benton Bank end of Jesmond Road, opposite Jesmond Dene Road.

Jesmond Parish Church
Consecrated in 1861

Designed by John Dobson. It was built in memory of Richard Clayton (1802-1856), a great Christian leader on Tyneside in the last century. The congregation is young. There is a strong emphasis on worship, prayer and learning. The sermons are intended to be relevant but biblical. There is also a strong emphasis on evangelism and fellowship. It is a church where you can bring your friends, whether agnostic or believing. Without pressure, agnostics will be encouraged to discover Jesus Christ as Lord and Saviour; believers, it is hoped, will be taught to think and act Christianly.

Times of Sunday Services:
8.00 a.m. Holy Communion (2nd, 4th and 5th Sundays)
10.45 a.m. Holy Communion (1st Sunday), Morning Prayer (2nd Sunday), Family Service (3rd Sunday), Morning Prayer (4th and 5th Sundays)
6.30 p.m. Evening Prayer (1st, 2nd, 4th and 5th Sundays) – Holy Communion (3rd Sunday)
Telephone: Vicarage – Newcastle 812001/812139
Road Location: Next to Jesmond Metro Station, Eskdale Terrace, Jesmond.

St. George's Church, Jesmond
Consecrated in 1888

A local shipbuilder, Charles Mitchell, appointed his shipyard architect, Thomas Ralph Spence, to design and build St. George's. The result is a church that cannot easily be labelled, with a splendid Italianate tower dominating Jesmond and an ornate chancel, bapistry and roof of great artistic merit: the use of tile and mosaic in the style of Art Nouveau is particularly striking. The organ is one of the best in the diocese and the musical tradition continues in the context of the Family Communion. Today's congregation aims for friendliness and acceptance to complement the imposing architecture.

Times of Sunday Services:
8.00 a.m. and 11.30 a.m. Holy Communion
9.30 a.m. The Family Communion
6.00 p.m. Evensong
Telephone: Vicarage – 811628
Parish Office – 811659
Road Location: St. George's Close, off Osborne Road, Jesmond.

St. Hilda's Church, Jesmond
Consecrated in 1905

St. Hilda's was built as a daughter church of St. George's when the houses and flats were built in 'West Jesmond (for people who were mainly railway workers) when the railway began to expand. The Parish was formed in 1909, four years after its Consecration. The church features a 'Hanging Pyx' in the Lady Chapel – the only one in the Diocese. A special feature is a War Memorial Triptych, painted by F. H. Newbury, with The Virgin and Jesus, Saint Hilda, Cullercoats Fishwife, a Miner, Engineer, Shipman, St. Nicholas, Roman Centurion, Norman King-Knight, Sailor, Soldier. Restoration with nave sanctuary carried out in 1981.

Times of Sunday Services:
7.30 a.m. Mattins (said)
8.00 a.m. Communion
9.30 a.m. Parish Communion
12.00 noon Communion
6.30 p.m. Evensong
Telephone: Vicarage – Newcastle 813130
Road Location: Thornleigh Road, Jesmond, Newcastle.

St. Barnabas' and St. Judes' Church, Sandyford
Dedicated in 1978

The parishes of St. Barnabas' and St. Jude's were united in 1974 and the Church Centre, the modernised former St. Barnabas' Hall, was dedicated in 1978. It comprises a church seating 50 or more, adaptable as a meeting room or church lounge; the main hall for recreation and services or meetings for up to 200; three classrooms; kitchen and toilets; a small vestry/projection room. This economical and flexible building is 'home' for a small, warm and active fellowship. We focus on the Word of God, which reveals Christ's salvation and gives strength and guidance for the Christian life.

Times of Sunday Services:
10.15 a.m. Holy Communion or Morning Prayer
6.30 p.m. Evening Prayer
Telephone: Vicarage – 0632 327837
Road Location: Greystoke Avenue, Sandyford

DO YOU PAY MORE THAN **£62.50** A YEAR RENTAL FOR YOUR COLOUR TELEVISION?

If so you should buy one from

MICHAEL PARRISH

and he will give you

1. A full 4-year guarantee on parts and labour
2. £100 part exchange on that set for a new set after 4 years

e.g.

PHILIPS 1002 22″ COLOUR TV
complete with stand and full 4 year guarantee **£350**

Less £100 part exchange
after 4 years **£100**

£250

Divide by 4 – **£62.50**

Compare these figures with rental charges and you can see it makes sense to buy from ...

MICHAEL PARRISH

OPENING HOURS:
Mon, Tues, Wed, Fri, Sat – 9 am - 5.30 pm
Thursday late night 7.30 pm

WHY NOT PAY BY OUR THREE CHEQUE SYSTEM

St. Bartholomew's Church, Benton

NEWCASTLE EAST DEANERY

St, Mark, Byker
Consecrated in 1906

The parish of St. Mark's, Byker came into being in 1904, although the present building was not completed until 1906. It is a parish which has sought to maintain a Bible based ministry. In recent years the large scale redevelopment of the area has considerably reduced the size of the parish population. The church itself has been extensively altered to incorporate a hall at the rear of the building and meeting rooms and other facilities in the south aisle.

Times of Sunday Services:
10.45 a.m. Morning Prayer
 6.30 p.m. Evening Prayer
10.45 a.m. Holy Communion (1st Sunday)
 6.30 p.m. Holy Communion (3rd Sunday)
And other times as announced
Telephone: Newcastle 656912
Road Location: Shields Road, Byker.

St. Martin's Church, Byker
Consecrated in 1933

The people of St. Martin's are lucky to have a warm, compact building in which to meet. It includes a church, seating for about 130, a screened-off chapel and a small hall. It is set in pleasant grounds which conceal a secluded vicarage. The people of St. Martin's mostly live close to the church. They are a lively, warm and prayerful people, with a tradition of service to their inner-city parish. St. Martin's was given a parish as recently as 1976, having been originally a daughter-church of St. Michael's, Byker. Today the parish boundaries extend from the Fossway to Dunstanburgh Road, and from Canterbury Street to Scrogg Road, and embrace about 7,000 souls.

Times of Sunday Services:
9.30 a.m. Parish Communion
3.15 p.m. Evening Prayer
Telephone: Vicarage – 0632 655931
Road Location: Near junction of Roman Avenue and Welbeck Road.

St. Michael with St. Lawrence, Byker
Consecrated in 1863

The Industrial Revolution transformed Byker within 60 years from a quiet little village into a large and rapidly expanding town of over 40,000 people. In 1853 Sir Matthew Ridley sold an acre of land as a site for Byker Parish Church, and the building was consecrated on 11 March 1863. The architecture is in the 'Decorated' style, and the building has a pleasant, well-proportioned interior. The north aisle was added in 1936, using materials from the then recently demolished St. Peter's Church in Oxford Street, Newcastle. The organ, a large 3-manual Binns, also came from St. Peter's, and is a fine instrument. The church, with its imposing 79-foot spire, is set on what is believed to be the highest point in Newcastle, and is thus a prominent landmark in the East end. More than £50,000 has been spent on the church in recent years, to preserve its use for many years to come in the new Byker housing development.

Times of Sunday Services:
8.00 a.m. Holy Communion
9.15 a.m. Parish Eucharist
6.00 p.m. Evensong
Telephone: Vicarage – Newcastle 653720
Road Location: Situated by the Byker Community Centre on Headlam Street, Byker.

St. Silas' Church, Byker
Consecrated in 1886

The church was designed by Johnson, the Diocesan architect, a fourth aisle was never added. The south side of the church is the most pleasing; a vestry building was added in 1930, and further extensions to this should be completed in 1982. The interior is well balanced architecturally. The organ and north aisle were destroyed by fire in 1970, and have been replaced; the organ is a much admired 'Collins'. Mr. L. Evetts designed and made the stained glass in the chancel based on Isaiah 6 1-8 and a Eurcharistic theme in memory of the late F. Davison (Vicar 74-77).

Times of Sunday Services:
9.15 a.m. Holy Communion
3.30 p.m. Evensong
Telephone: Vicarage – 0632 655353
Road Location: Clifford Street near top of Byker Bank (station Byker Metro).

St. Gabriel's Church, Heaton
Dedicated in 1899

The parish of St. Gabriel was formed in 1900 out of St. Michael, Byker. The architect of the church was Frank Rich and the builder Walter Baston. The building was completed by 1932. The tower was 99 ft high. The interior is spacious. The nave is dominated by a rood and the east end has a large triptych, topped by the figure of Christ in majesty. Above it is a large mural painting of the Ascension. There is a Lady Chapel, where there is a copy of the Bishop's Bible of 1568, and a chapel dedicated to St. Andrew. The church is open throughout the day.

Times of Sunday Services:
8.00 a.m. Holy Communion
9.15 a.m. Holy Communion
11.00 a.m. Holy Communion
6.30 p.m. Evensong
Telephone: Vicarage – Newcastle 655843
Road Location: Junction of St. Gabriel's Avenue with Heaton Road.

St. Francis' Church, High Heaton
Dedicated in 1953
Built at a time of post-war building restrictions the church is an interesting example of simple construction and use of light to focus all attention on the altar.
Times of Sunday Services:
8.00 a.m. Holy Communion
9.00 a.m. Parish Communion
6.30 p.m. Evensong
Telephone: Vicarage – Newcastle 661071
Road Location: Top of Cleveland Gardens – High Heaton (behind the Freeman Hospital).

St. Bartholomew's Church, Benton
Rebuilt 1791
The church is of particular interest for its early gothic revival tower and spire, a well proportioned composition of 1790. The later Victorian Gothic work, 'lancet' in the chancel and 'perpendicular' in the south aisle with its attractive porch, is pleasing work of its period. The spacious interior contains a font of 1857 with floral and heraldic carving, an interesting series of mural tablets, and two of the earliest ledger stones in the county, dated 1581 and 1587. The polygonal church hall of 1980 is a striking example of modern design and function blending with those of an earlier period.

Times of Sunday Services:
 7.30 a.m. Mattins
 8.00 a.m. Holy Eucharist
 9.15 a.m. Parish Eucharist
11.00 a.m. Sung Eucharist
 6.00 p.m. Evensong
Telephone: Vicarage – 662015
Road Location: Station Road, Benton.

St. Mary Magdalene, Longbenton
Consecrated on Sunday 28 July 1957
The church is situated in the centre of Longbenton Estate. Negotiations for building began in 1952 and the Consecration was in 1957. In the patronage of Balliol College, the first Vicar was Instituted in 1970, when the daughter became a Parish and Sister.

The updated font (replaced in 1857), served as a sundial support in the Parish churchyard until restored in St. Mary's, a link with time past, and symbol of rebirth.

The bell which once summoned children to study at Longbenton Church School, was acquired, and now calls the family to share in worship and service at St. Mary Magdalene.
Times of Sunday Services:
8.00 a.m. Holy Communion (said)
9.00 a.m. Holy Communion (sung)
Telephone: Vicarage – 662326
Road Location: West Farm Avenue, Longbenton.

Christ Church, Walker
Consecrated in 1848

Christ Church was formed out of the parish of St. Bartholomew, Longbenton, in 1848. It lays claim to having the largest churchyard in the country, with 11 acres. Within the parish there are the famous Tyneside shipyards. The great west window in the church, depicting Christ in glory surrounded by some of the Northern saints, was erected in memory of a member of a local shipyard family. The chapel in the north aisle was furnished from the now demolished church of St. Cuthbert, Newcastle.

Times of Sunday Services:
8.00 a.m. Holy Communion
9.30 a.m. Parish Communion
6.30 p.m. Evensong
Telephone: Vicarage – Wallsend 623666
Road Location: Churchwalk Shopping Centre, Church Street, Walker.

St. Anthony of Egypt, Walker
Dedicated in 1868

The church was built by Lord Northbourne to serve the industrial village on the banks of the Tyne. The area has been known as St. Anthony's since the late Middle Ages. The name therefore had to be preserved, but the dedication was to St. Anthony of Egypt, because the RC Church of St. Anthony of Padua was already in Walker. Since the 1920s, vast housing estates have covered what were once fields, and there is a population of over 12,000. A Church primary school serves the parish.

Times of Sunday Services:
8.00 a.m. Mass
9.30 a.m. Parish Mass
6.00 p.m. Solemn Evensong and Benediction
6.45 p.m. Mass
Telephone: Vicarage – Newcastle 651605
Road Location: Belmont Street, St. Anthony's, Walker.

St. Oswald's Church, Walkergate
Consecrated in 1932

The church of St. Oswald, Walkergate was built in 1932 to meet the spiritual and fellowship needs of large building extensions from Walker in the Walkergate, Walkerville and Daisy Hill area and to serve a population of over 12,000 people. Two halls built one over the other, it was intended later to build a new church nearby, but this was never started. The lower hall has been adapted and made into a very lovely church with all the furnishings given in memory of parishioners. This together with a new youth centre makes St. Oswald's a very workable and complete parish unit.

Times of Sunday Services:
9.30 a.m. Holy Communion
11.00 a.m. Children and Family Service
6.30 p.m. Evensong
Telephone: Vicarage – Newcastle 623662
Road Location: Woodhead Road, Walkergate, Newcastle 6.

St. Mary the Virgin, Ponteland.

ꟾNEWCASTLE WEST ꟾDEANERY

Inner West

St. James' Church, Benwell
Consecrated in 1832
Erected as Chapel of ease in the Parochial Chapter of St. John in the Parish of St. Nicholas. Architect John Dobson.

1843 Parish of Benwell formed, extensive rural area, large private houses population 1,600.

1880 church extended, 1895 steeple, clock, porch, baptistry. 1903 north aisle added.

1980 south aisle converted into Church Hall.

Note: pointed roof beams, pulpit, screens, peel of 8 bells, grave of Richard Grainger famous city developer; of former vicars — 4 became Bishops, 2 Archdeacons.

Times of Sunday Services:
  8.00 a.m. Holy Communion
10.00 a.m. Family Eucharist
  6.30 p.m. Evensong
Telephone: Vicarage — Newcastle 735021
Road Location: Benwell Lane, Newcastle upon Tyne.

Venerable Bede, Benwell
Consecrated in 1937
The church was built in 1936/37 to replace a smaller, wooden building that had existed from the start of the century. Originally established as a Mission church springing from St. James', Benwell, its status is now that of a district church, which means it functions as a parish church though in federation with St. James and St. John's in Benwell. The building was designed by Prof. W. B. Edwards and is typical of churches built in the pre-war era with tiled roofs and detailed brickwork.

Times of Sunday Services:
  8.00 a.m. Holy Communion
10.00 a.m. Family Communion
11.15 a.m. Sunday School
  6.30 p.m. Evensong
Telephone: Vicarage — Newcastle 735356
Road Location: Corner of Westgate Road and Benwell Grove.

St. John the Baptist Church, Benwell Village
Dedicated 12 September 1950

In 1820, St. John's Church in Grainger Street established a Sunday School in Benwell Village. After the formation of Benwell Parish the School was taken over by St. James'. At a later date services were begun and St. John's became a daughter church. In 1941 a severe storm wrecked the building. Communion Services were then held in the Bishop's Chapel at Benwell Towers until the erection of a new building in 1949/50. This was dedicated by Bishop Hudson on 12 September 1950. It is a dual purpose building, the Sanctuary being shut off by folding doors when the hall is used for secular activities.

Times of Sunday Services:
9.00 a.m. Holy Communion
Telephone: Church Committee Secretary – Miss M. P. Cross – Newcastle 742427
Road Location: West Road – Pease Avenue (opposite Two Ball Lonnen) into Benwell Village.

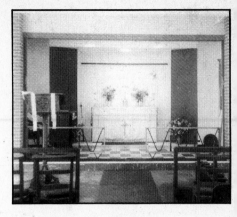

St. Peter's Church, Cowgate
Consecrated in 1953

As Newcastle began to expand in the 1920s with new houses being built along the roads into town, the Church Army with members of local churches visited the new homes in Cowgate, and services were held in some. In 1928 a dual-purpose building was erected and dedicated to the Holy Trinity. By 1945 a new building was needed, the first stage of which was consecrated in 1953 and dedicated to St. Peter. It has never been completed. It is a building of no architectural merit and yet because of its interior appointment makes an attractive building for worship, the focal point being the Christus Rex carved by Kathleen Parbury on Lindisfarne.

Times of Sunday Services:
8.00 a.m. Holy Communion
9.30 a.m. Sung Eucharist
6.00 p.m. Evensong
Telephone: Vicarage – Newcastle 869913
Road Location: The west side of the A6127 at Cowgate.

Holy Cross Church, Fenham
Consecrated in 1936

Holy Cross, Fenham, was built by John Blackett-Ord of Whitfield on land which he provided. His family had lived in Fenham Hall for some generations and owned much of the land in Fenham. The church was dedicated on Holy Cross Day, September 14 1936. In 1965 Mr. Blackett-Ord added a porch in memory of his wife Mary. The church is built of old brick and is of the utmost simplicity architecturally. Inside a huge crucifix hangs on the wall, high up, at the east end of the building. Externally the church is conspicuous for its NW tower, on the top of which is a large gilded cross.

Times of Sunday Services:
8.00 a.m. Holy Communion
9.30 a.m. Parish Communion
6.30 p.m. Evensong
Telephone: Newcastle 744476
Road Location: Church lies between Ovington Grove and Whittington Grove.

St. Augustine of Hippo, Fenham
Consecrated on 16 June 1892

Main body of church beautifully proportioned, 1892 chancel and lady chapel added 1907 — both spacious the former of great dignity and restrained enchantment to Anglican form of worship. The lady chapel equally attractive and devotional. East window adorned with the four latin fathers, Ambrose, Augustine, Gregory and Jerome centred on the 'Ascension'. The upper lights of the chancel dedicated to the early church martyrs.

Beautiful wrought iron work between chancel and chapel, two fine oak choir screens 1914-1918 and 1939-1945. NB upper light in main church with theme of early English saints. Splendid *te deum* window glowing on the whole church from the west end. The church in the main owes its form of beauty and presence to the care, work and generosity of George Miles, priest, vicar, for 46 years from 6 months after its foundation until his death in 1939.

Times of Sunday Services:
8.00 a.m. Holy Communion (said)
9.30 a.m. Holy Communion (sung)
8.45 a.m. Mattins
6.00 p.m. Evensong
Telephone: Vicarage — Newcastle 735859
Road Location: Brighton Grove.

St. James and St. Basil's Church, Fenham
Consecrated in 1931

Worship began in Fenham in the 1890s in the north chapel of the cemetery. From there it moved to St. Monicas, and finally to the present church. Sir James Knott paid for the building of the church in memory of his two sons, James and Basil both killed in the First World War. The church is built from stones taken from the old Newcastle Prison, which was being demolished at the time. The architect was E. E. Lofting and the stained glass the work of Edward Moore. The organ was designed and built for the church by J. W. Walker and Sons and contains a 'floating celestial division'.

Times of Sunday Services:
8.00 a.m. Holy Communion
9.30 a.m. Holy Communion (sung)
6.30 p.m. Evensong and Sermon
Telephone: Vicarage — Newcastle 745078
Road Location: The north-west corner of the junction of Wingrove Road and Fenham Hall Drive.

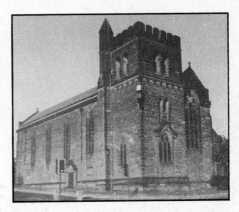

St. Paul's Church, High Elswick
Consecrated in 1858

Elswick is an urban redevelopment area, with council housing rebuilt during the seventies. St. Paul's is the only Christian denomination in the parish, the only other building used for religious purposes is the Mosque. The church hall was leased to the City Council in 1977 to be used as a Community Centre. Sunday services are held in the church vestry during the winter, while much of the church's evangelistic work goes on in local home groups.

Times of Sunday Services:
9.30 a.m. Holy Communion
11.15 a.m. (last Sunday of month)
6.30 p.m. Evening Prayer
Telephone: Vicarage — Newcastle 734705
Road Location: Havelock Street lies just north of Elswick Road between Elswick Road and the West Road; ¼ mile west of the junction of Elswick Road with Westgate Hill known as the Big Lamp.

St. Philip's Church, High Elswick
Consecrated in 1873

The church was built as a national memorial to Archbishop Longley, who is also commemorated in a local street name: Longley was translated to the Bishopric of Durham in 1856 and then after two years as Archbishop of York was appointed to Canterbury in 1862. During his primacy he established the Lambeth Conferences: he died in 1868, the year in which it was decided to build a church in a new parish to be formed in High Elswick. In recent years most of the original housing has been replaced with modern terraces and flats.

Times of Sunday Services:
9.30 a.m. Parish Communion and Sunday School
6.00 p.m. Evensong
Telephone: Vicarage – 737407
Road Location: St. Philip's Close, off Douglas Terrace.

St. Stephen's Church, Low Elswick
Dedicated in 1868

The foundation stone was laid by Sir W. G. Armstrong on 19 November 1866 and the church was dedicated by the Lord Bishop of Durham. Donations to meet the cost of £5,700 came from various sources including £500 from the Elswick firm of Sir W. G. Armstrong and £900 from Bishop Baring's Special Church Building Fund. The Cruddas family too were generous and faithful benefactors (W. D. Cruddas was churchwarden from 1866-1912). They contributed the tower and spire, north aisle, large vestry, west porch and the peal of 8 bells. The chancel houses a fine oak reredos depiciting the last supper and an organ which was given by Sir William Armstrong in 1868.

Times of Sunday Services:
10.30 a.m. Morning Prayer/Holy Communion (alternating morn/eve)
6.30 p.m. Evening Prayer/Holy Communion
10.30 a.m. Family Service/Parade service (1st Sun in month)
Telephone: Vicarage – Newcastle 734680
Road Location: Bordering on Scotswood Road, Clumber Street and Brunel Terrace.

St. Matthew's Church, 'Big Lamp', Newcastle
Consecrated in 1867

The present building, completed in 1905, reflects in its design, proportions and workmanship the taste and wealth of the professional classes which then abounded in the area (for artisans St. Wilfred's Mission was established elsewhere in the parish) and the whole of the very large tower complete with its 8 bells (tenor 31¼ cwt) was the gift of a single benefactor.

Accoustically, the building is impressive and great store is set upon maintaining, to the best of local ability, a fully sung Service (in a firmly tractarian tradition) on Sundays and important Holy Days.

Times of Sunday Services:
9.30 a.m. Mass (sung)
11.30 a.m., 7.30 p.m. Low Mass (All Rite B)
6.30 p.m. Evensong (1662)
Telephone: Vicarage – (0632) 322866
Road Location: Situated at the junction of Elswick and Westgate Roads, the church is on major bus routes (services 30, 31, 33, 34, 35, 38), but can be reached by car only by way of Houston Street which leads off Rye Hill immediately to the south of St. Paul's School playing fields.

74

**St. Margaret (of Antioch), Scotswood
Consecrated in 1918**
Building begun in 1915. Consecrated by Bishop Wild. Pillars and arches of Denwick Stone, red-tiled roof, with oak spirelet. 126 feet long nave, with north and south aisles and baptistry. Replaced an earlier building.
Times of Sunday Services:
8.00 a.m. Holy Communion
9.15 a.m. Family Communion
6.00 p.m. Evensong
Telephone: Vicarage — Newcastle 746322
Road Location: Corner of Armstrong Road, Denton Road (the Ring Road) and Heighley Street.

Outer West

**St. Cuthbert's Church, Blucher
Year of dedication: 1905**
Built by the Spencer's Steel Manufacturer Newburn as a daughter church of Newburn to serve Blucher villagers.
Times of Sunday Services:
9.00 a.m. Holy Communion (3rd Sundays)
6.00 p.m. Evening Prayer
Telephone: Vicarage — Lemington 670958
Road Location: On A69 in Blucher Village.

**Church of the Holy Nativity, Chapel House
Consecrated in 1972**
The church began its life in the vicarage where services and organisations as they were formed were held for eighteen months. The Church Hall came into use in 1967 and services were held there until the opening of the church. This modern brick built building contains some wrought iron sculptures by Charles Sansbury of Allendale. The foyer contains a stylised form of the Star of Bethlehem, the centre of which represents the folds of the swathling clothes wrapped round the infant Jesus at His nativity. The star theme is continued in the main sculpture on the east wall which continues the nativity theme and also the death, resurrection and ascension of Jesus. There are other, smaller examples of Mr. Sansbury's work in this attractive, modern building. Architect Mr. John Kirkham.
Times of Sunday Services:
 8.00 a.m. Holy Communion
 9.30 a.m. Family Communion
11.00 a.m. Children's Church
 6.30 p.m. Evensong
Telephone: Vicarage — Newcastle 674069
Road Location: Hillhead Parkway

Holy Trinity Church, Dalton
Consecrated in 1837
Built as a chapel of ease to Newburn by the Collingwood family of Dissington Hall. Architect Green of Newcastle who was responsible for the Theatre Royal, Grey Street, Newcastle. They also built Holy Saviour, Sugley about the same time and there are striking similarities of design, the square nave and shallow chancel before the neo Gothic of the Victorian era. The church is very much as originally built and furnished. There are two hatchments of Collingwood family.
Times of Sunday Services:
  2.35 p.m. Evening Prayer (Oct-Mar – Alternate Sundays)
                 (Apr-Sept – every Sunday)
Holy Communion 2nd Sunday
Telephone: Vicarage – Lemington 670958
Road Location: Dalton Village.

Church of the Holy Spirit, Denton
Consecrated in 1956
The red brick building which serves a parish of approximately 17,000 people was built by Messrs Stephen Eastern Ltd and designed by the Architects Newcombe and Newcombe. The design of the Kelham Chapel, built for the Society of the Sacred Mission in 1928 has a considerable influence on the building.

The church was consecrated on 13 October 1956 and replaced the Mission Church/Hall built in 1865 on the West Road. In 1966 a Narthex was added and in 1980 a new Hall, linked to the church, complements the church building.
Times of Sunday Services:
8.00 a.m. Holy Communion
9.30 a.m. Sung Eucharist
6.30 p.m. Evening Prayer
Telephone: Vicarage – Newcastle 674376
Road Location: Dunblane Crescent. North of West Road after Denton Burn Roundabout (going west).

Holy Saviour, Milbourne
Consecrated in 1871
The foundation stone of the Chapel of ease of the Milbourne Estate was laid on 15 May 1867 by Miss Jane Anne Bates, eldest daughter of Ralph Bates, JP, DL.

The building, a fine unspoilt example of Victorian Gothic and able to seat 100 people, consists of chancel, nave, vestry and porch.

An interesting external feature is the broach spire. Internally, the wall lights are the original oil lamps now lit by electricity. The bells and clock in the tower were given by Nathaniel Bates, and the altar cloth, communion rail cushions and hassocks were worked and given by Miss Sarah Bates.
Time of Sunday Service:
11.15 a.m. Every Sunday, Eucharist with hymns and address
Telephone: Vicarage – Ponteland (0661) 22140
Road Location: Milbourne Village is two miles from a left turn on the A.696 two miles north-west of Ponteland.

St. Wilfrid's Church, Newbiggin Hall
Dedicated in 1967

St. Wilfrid's Church was built to serve the new housing estates of Newbiggin Hall, Whorlton Grange, Etal Park and Cheviot View on the western outskirts of the city. The church building is square in design with the altar at one corner and seating in a semi-circle around the altar. The design of the building lends itself to worship in the Catholic tradition that is both dignified and relaxed, and emphasises the participation of the whole congregation. One of the special features of the church is the set of wood carved stations of the cross.

Times of Sunday Services:
8.00 a.m. Eucharist
9.30 a.m. Parish Eucharist
6.30 p.m. Evening Prayer
Telephone: Vicarage — Newcastle 860343
Road Location: Trevelyan Drive, Newbiggin Hall.

St. Michael and All Angels, Newburn
Consecrated in 1170

Replaced a Saxon church burnt down 1070. Saxon/Norman tower. Nave: N. aisle Norman; S. aisle transitional; choir early English thirteenth century. Internal restoration 1885. There is a 'weeping chancel', an unusual Eastern sepulchre. Association with George Stephenson the engineer and Thomas Hedley locomotive engineer and father of the principle benefactor of the Diocese in 1880s. Registers go back to 1657. The tower featured as a gun platform in battle of Newburn 1640.

Times of Sunday Services:
10.15 a.m. Holy Communion (3rd Sunday)
10.15 a.m. Morning Prayer (1st and 4th Sundays)
        Family Service (2nd Sunday)
      6.15 p.m. Evening Prayer
Holy Communion (1st Sunday BCP used)
Telephone: Vicarage — Lemington 670958
Road Location: Centre of Newburn.

St. Mary the Virgin, Ponteland
Consecrated about 1150

Though a Saxon grave-marker still remains in the church the earliest surviving parts of the present building are Norman: this is the date of the tower, with its fine west doorway, and part of the nave arcade. We owe the north transept, with its buttressed lancet windows, and part of the chancel to a large re-building programme in the thirteenth century. By this stage the church was aisled. Signs are that the aisles were widened in the fifteenth century. There were a series of restorations in the 19th century whilst the liturgical reorganisation of the 1970s has brought a central altar to the crossing. Among noteable fittings are fourteenth century glass, a pre-Reformation bell and a royal arms of 1815-1837. The registers date back to 1602.

Times of Sunday Services:
  8.00 a.m. Holy Communion with address
9.25 a.m. Sung Eucharist with address
6.30 p.m. Evensong with sermon
Telephone: Vicarage — Ponteland (0661) 22140
           Vestry Office — Ponteland (0661) 24470
           Road Location: Centre of Ponteland.

Holy Saviour, Sugley
Dedicated in 1837

The church was designed by Benjamin Green of Newcastle who also designed Dalton Church and the Theatre Royal, Newcastle. The foundation stone was laid on 24 June 1836 by Mr. Charles Bulmer. A William IV silver coin was placed in a glass vessel and sunk in the foundations. The church is built in Early English style and runs north to south instead of the usual east to west due to the existence of a disused pit shaft on the east side. It was built as a chapel of ease to Newburn Parish Church and became a separate parish fifty years later in 1887.

Times of Sunday Services:
8.00 a.m. and 9.15 a.m. Holy Communion
6.00 p.m. Evening Prayer
Telephone: Vicarage — 674633
Road Location: Corner of Newburn Road and Tyne View, Lemington.

St. Mary's Church, Throckley
Year of Dedication 1887

The cost of the building was partly defrayed out of a gift made to the Bishop of Newcastle's fund, by John Spencer of Newburn Steel Works for the requirements of Newburn Parish the remainder of the cost being an offering by John Spencer of Whorlton Hall to this parish in memory of his wife who died in 1882.

Times of Sunday Services:
10.30 a.m. Family Service
 6.00 p.m. Evening Prayer
 8.00 a.m. Holy Communion (1st Sunday)
 9.15 a.m. Holy Communion (4th Sunday) and as announced
9.15 a.m. Morning Prayer (2nd and 3rd Sundays)
Telephone: Vicarage — Lemington 674553
Road Location: Throckley Roundabout. Corner of Hexham Road and Newburn Road.

St. John's Church, Whorlton
Consecrated in 1899

Consecrated in 1899 as a chapel of ease in the parish of Newburn, the church stood for many years in rural isolation well away from the mining community of Westerhope it was built to serve, until recent years when it has been surrounded by new housing estates.

Earlier this century a new and larger chancel was added to the existing building with the intention of adding side aisles and raising the roof of the original chapel.

The onset of war and lack of funds has resulted in the interesting but aesthetically displeasing present combination of bricked up stonework! St. John's is part of the Whorlton Team Ministry.

Times of Sunday Services:
8.10 a.m. Holy Communion
9.20 a.m. Family Communion
Telephone: Vicarage — Newcastle 869648
Road Location: Stamfordham Road, Westerhope. B6324 Nr junction with North Walbottle Road.

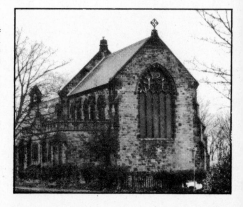

Saint Wilfrid's Church, Newbiggin Hall Estate.

Holy Nativity, Chapel House.

Saint George's Church, Cullercoats.

TYNEMOUTH DEANERY

St. Peter's Church, Balkwell
Consecrated in 1938

Opened in 1938, the present church of St. Peter took its title from a church of the same name on the New Quay, North Shields which closed in 1936.

The building replaced the Balkwell Mission built in 1930 and indeed that building now forms part of the church complex.

Whilst having a rather austere exterior, the true beauty of the building can be appreciated on entry when the visitor is struck by the splendid boarded ceiling with its supporting beams blending well with the brickwork interior. The view facing east is dominated by the central rood.

Times of Sunday Services:
8.00 a.m. Holy Communion
9.15 a.m. Sung Eucharist
9.15 a.m. Sunday School
6.30 p.m. Sung Evensong
Telephone: Vicarage — North Shields 570952
Road Location: At the junction of Central Avenue and the Quadrant.

St. John Baptist, Backworth

This small but graceful stone church was built in 1886 by the Taylor family of Chipchase Castle. It is in the parish of Earsdon but until 1955 it always had a priest-in-charge who lived in the clergy house near the church. The last priest-in-charge was Rev. A. Wilson, now Canon at the Cathedral. St. John's is probably unique in that at one time it was in a different deanery to the parish church at Earsdon. One was in Bedlington deanery and one in Tynemouth deanery. They are both now correctly in Tynemouth deanery. Since 1955 the vicar of St. Alban's, Earsdon, has looked after St. John's.

Times of Sunday Services:
8.00 a.m. Holy Communion
6.00 p.m. Evening Prayer
Alternate months in conjunction with Earsdon
Telephone: Vicarage — Whitley Bay 529393
Road Location: Backworth.

St. Aidan's Church, Billy Mill
Dedicated in 1958

In 1951 a small group of people from the Lynn Estate and Chirton Grange became the nucleus of a worshipping community at Billy Mill. The results of the community's effort can be seen today. The church hall is a witness to the time and energy consumed and given. The hall and a chapel for smaller services were dedicated by the Bishop of Newcastle in 1955. They then began to collect funds for a room to be the church which was dedicated in 1958. In 1976 the church was extended. The worshipping area has been transformed and the atmosphere of the building is one of unobtrusive modernity. The cross on the east wall of the sanctuary was a gift from the people of St. George's, Cullercoats. The Sanctuary Lamp and Aumbrey on the south wall were the gift of the people of St. Hilda's, Marden.

Times of Sunday Services:
8.00 a.m. Holy Communion
9.30 a.m. Parish Communion
Telephone: Vicarage — North Shields 573616
Road Location: Billy Mill Lane, North Shields.

St. George's Church, Cullercoats
Consecrated 1884

Built by the 6th Duke of Northumberland in 1884. Architect J. L. Pearson. Perfectly proportioned Gothic building, stone vaulted and finished with great attention to detail. Tower and spire 180 feet high. Building matched to its splendid, but exposed, coastal site. Its architectural perfection is statement of what it stands for — the glory of God — and the worship of the faithful. The furnishings and the hand-made kneelers are all part of the offering of praise to God by His people.

Times of Sunday Services:
8.00 a.m. Holy Communion
9.30 a.m. Parish Eucharist
6.30 p.m. Evensong and Sermon
Telephone: Whitley Bay Vicarage — 521817
Road Location: A193 between Tynemouth and Whitley Bay on the sea front.

St. Hilda's Church, Marden with Preston Grange

Dedicated on 21 December 1966. It is a modern Church showing a French influence in the architecture. The formation of the Cullercoats Team Ministry in March 1975 was an important step in the life of St. Hilda's. From being a daughter Church to St. George's, Cullercoats, it became part of a 3-Church team ministry with St. George's and St. Aidan's, Billy Mill, each Church having its own Vicar.

The Church was consecrated on St. Hilda's Day, 17 November 1976 and serves a parish of 8,000.

Times of Sunday Services:
8.00 a.m. Holy Communion
9.00 a.m. Parish Communion
11.15 a.m. Sunday School
6.30 p.m. Evensong
Telephone: Vicarage — North Shields 576595
Road Location: East along A1058 (dual carriageway, cost road) and single carriageway continuation to indoor swimming pool. Turn left onto A192 (dual carriageway, Preston Road).

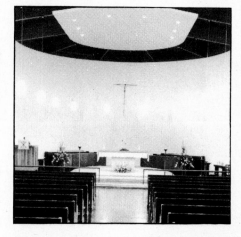

St. Alban's Church, Earsdon
Consecrated in 1837

The name Earsdon is derived from the much earlier name of Erdesdun (hill of red earth). Before 1250 the church was under the care of the monks of Tynemouth Priory who in their turn were ruled from the great Benedictine Monastery at St. Alban's. This could explain how Earsdon's Church became dedicated to the first British Martyr. On 12 January 1862 occured the deadful Hartley Mine disaster. The memorial stone to the 204 victims can be easily found at the north-east side of the church. In 1874 Lord Hastings of Delaval Hall presented two lancet windows. His Lordship obtained the glass from Hampton Court Palace in 1840. It is believed to have been made originally by the famous Galyon Hone in 1531 at the order of King Henry VIII. Traces of Tudor crests and arms can be clearly seen. Our unique super frontal was made by a parishioner in memory of her parents, and in honour of all the saints. The saints dipicted represent the churches in Whitley Bay, Shiremoor, Earsdon and Backworth – (6) and four saints of the North of England – Northumbria.

The Royal coat of arms positioned on the balcony of the church was unveiled on Thursday 16 June 1977.

Times of Sunday Eervices:
10.00 a.m. The Eucharist (sung)
  6.00 p.m. alternate months with Backworth
Telephone: Vicarage – Whitley Bay529393
Road Location: Village of Earsdon.

St. Mary the Virgin, Monkseaton
Consecrated in 1931

Formerly a daughter church of St. Paul, Whitley Bay, St. Mary's became a separate parish in the 1920s and the church was consecrated on 5 December 1931. The church was further extended to include a baptistry and entrance vestibule in 1964. The modern church hall was completed in the early 1960s. The church has a modern Allen computer organ.

Times of Sunday Services:
 8.00 a.m. Holy Communion
 9.15 a.m. Parish Communion
10.45 a.m. Holy Communion
 6.00 p.m. Evensong
Telephone: Vicarage – Whitley Bay 522484
Road Location: At the junction of Davison Avenue and Claremont Gardens.

St. Peter's Church, Monkseaton
Consecrated in 1938

Originally part of St. Paul, Whitley Bay. the church was dedicated on the Eve of the Feast of St. Peter in 1938 by Bishop Bilbrough. In 1939, it became a Parish in its own right. It was bombed during the war but was successfully repaired and is now an imposing red brick building containing two examples of modern stained glass designed by Mr. Evetts of Newcastle University. The Lady Chapel window is the War Memorial.

Times of Sunday Services:
 7.30 a.m. Mattins
 8.00 a.m. Holy Communion
 9.00 a.m. Parish Communion
11.30 a.m. Holy Communion
 6.00 p.m. Evensong
Telephone: Vicarage – Whitley Bay 521991
Road Location: Woodleigh Road.

St. Augustin's Church, North Shields
Consecrated on 18 Nov 1884 by Bishop John Wilberforce

Consecrated by Bishop Wilberforce on 18 November 1884: and was thus the first church to be consecrated in the new Diocese of Newcastle. The Chancel added in 1888; the Vestries in 1955; there are many handsome stained glass windows.

The oak pulpit originally stood in the Cathedral. It had been given to St. Nicholas' in 1878 by Charles Tully J.P. of Tynemouth and was given to the Parish when the present alabaster pulpit was erected in the Cathedral.

Tradition says that the bell was a ship's bell, rescued from a wreck and presented by the Captain's Widow.

Times of Sunday Services:
10.00 a.m. Family Communion (1st Sunday, Family Service)
6.00 p.m. Evensong (1st Sunday, Holy Communion)
Telephone: Vicarage – North Shields 571721
Road Location: Corner of Washington Terrance and Jackson Street near to Tynemouth Golf Course.

St Augustin's Church, NORTH SHIELDS

Christ Church
Tynemouth Parish Church
Consecrated in 1668

Although situated in North Shields, Christ Church was built to be the Parish Church of Tynemouth when Tynemouth Priory could no longer act as a Parish Church. The original cruciform church has grown over the years into a handsome building, almost square but with chancel and tower added. Its records go back to 1668. There is a peal of ten bells, and the organ, now in the west gallery, is said to have come from Vauxhall gardens. The seafaring links of Christ Church are preserved in the Mariners Chapel. The lovely modern glass, especially the east window, adds lightness and colour to this most unusual church.

Times of Sunday Services:
8.00 a.m. Holy Communion (series III)
10.00 a.m. Parish Communion with Sunday School (series III)
6.30 p.m. Evensong
Telephone: Vicarage – 0632 571721
Road Location: Preston Road, North Shields.

St. John's Church, Percy Main
Consecrated in 1864

The church was designed by the architect Sabrin for the Duke of Northumberland. It is a simple stone building with chancel, nave and two aisles, typical of many churches built in Northumberland at about the same period

Times of Sunday Services:
8.30 a.m. Holy Communion
9.30 a.m. Parish Communion
6.30 p.m. Evensong
Telephone: Vicarage – North Shields 571819
Road Location: St. John's Terrace, Percy Main.

St. Mark's Church, Shiremoor
Consecrated on 4 November 1967
Conventional district of St. John, Percy Main from 1890s until creation of present parish in 1967, when new church also opened. Modern polygonal design with free standing altar of Northumberland slate, congregational seating on three sides of altar. Designed for Westward facing celebration. Distinctive features, large parabolic curved east wall.
Times of Sunday Services:
8.00 a.m. Holy Communion (said)
9.30 a.m. Sung Eucharist
6.30 p.m. Evening Prayer (said)
Telephone: Vicarage – Whitley Bay 533291
Road Location: Brenkley Avenue, Shiremoor.

Holy Saviour, Tynemouth Priory
Consecrated in 1841
The parish church of Holy Saviour, Tynemouth Priory, was built to the designs of John and Benjamin Green, and consecrated on 11 August 1841. It served as a chapel of ease to Tynemouth Parish Church until 1861 when it was granted full parochial status. The first vicar, Thomas Featherstone, built Church Schools in 1869, later ceded to the L.E.A., in 1925. The church building was enlarged in 1884. Originally amid green fields, it now stands at the inter-section of seven roads like the hub of a great wheel, and is ideally placed as a centre of worship and mission.
Times of Sunday Services:
8.00 a.m. Holy Communion (said)
9.00 a.m. Mattins (said)
10.00 a.m. Family Eucharist (choral)
6.30 p.m. Evensong (choral)
Telephone: Vicarage – North Shields 571636
Road Location: Crossway, Tynemouth.

St. John the Evangelist, Wallsend
Consecrated in 1956
St. John's is firmly established in the Catholic tradition of the Anglican Church, with a daily celebration of Holy Communion, plus a special keeping of Saints' days. St. John's was gazetted a Parochial District with complete independence in June 1954, by the Queen in Council, and became a 'parish' when the present church was consecrated in 1956. Special feature: a fine 'Christus Rex' by Charles Sansbury of Allendale.
Times of Sunday Services:
7.30 p.m. Mattins
8.00 a.m. Holy Communion
9.30 a.m. Parish Communion
6.30 p.m. Evensong
Telephone: Vicarage – Wallsend 623944
Road Location: Station Road, Wallsend (100 yards south of Coast Road).

Saint Luke's Church, Wallsend
Consecrated in 1885

A grey stone towered building in early English Gothic, with a barrel vaulted nave, aisles, plain round pillars, and pointed arches. The chancel, tower and Lady chapel added at a later date all in the same style as nave.

The east window is a memorial to parishioners who died in the 1914-18 War. It is of surpassing beauty depicting the Crucifixion. Strong glowing colours are a feature of this window by Wilhelmina Geddes of Dublin (considered one of her finest creations). Another treasure of the church is a gilded chancel Angel screen.

Times of Sunday Services:
8.00 a.m. Eurcharist
9.30 a.m. Eucharist (sung; with creche for children)
7.30 p.m. Eucharist
8.00 a.m. Mattins
6.30 p.m. Evensong (sung)
Telephone: Vicarage – Wallsend 623723
Road Location: Junction of Station Road, Wallsend and Frank Street.

St. Peter's Church, Wallsend
Consecrated in 1809

The parish church of Wallsend built to replace the ancient church of the Holy Cross – the ruins of which are about half a mile distant. Originally a late-Georgian 'preaching box' the church was restored and Gothicised in the 1890s. Of special note are the windows in the north wall – Dublin glass of the 1920s – the central window is the work of W. Geddes (see S. Luke, Wallsend).

The churchyard contains numbers of nineteenth century headstones with typically sombre inscriptions whose gloom is offset by the two church schools – the oldest educational establishment in Wallsend, dating from 1833.

Times of Sunday Services:
9.30 a.m. Parish Mass
5.30 p.m. Evensong
Telephone: Vicarage – 0632 623852
Road Location: Church Bank, High Street East, Wallsend.

St. Paul's Church, Whitley Bay
Consecrated in 1864

Stone built Early English form furnished in traditional manner. There is a tower with a peel of eight bells and a curious trunncated spire. The church is set in a churchyard, now disused, forming a pleasant open space in the centre of the town.

Times of Sunday Services:
8.00 a.m. Holy Communion
10.00 a.m. Parish Communion
6.00 p.m. Evening Prayer
Telephone: Vicarage: Whitley Bay 524916
Road Location: Park View, Whitley Bay.

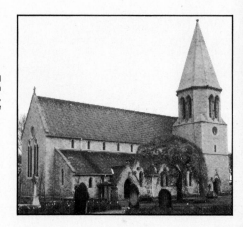

St. Mary the Virgin, Willington
Consecrated in 1876

Built in 1876 the building, which is architecturally typical of that era, served the small rural community of 1,535 within the concepts of that time. Now, surrounded by a population of over 27,000 it continues to serve the community in the same way but has incorporated within its attitude of caring, a practical attitude of helping others to attain personal fulfilment of their own peculiar and specific gifts and talents.

Times of Sunday Services:
8.15 a.m. Holy Communion
9.30 a.m. Parish Communion
6.30 p.m. Evensong
Telephone: Vicarage – Wallsend 628208
　　　　　　Office – Wallsend 625220
Road Location: Churchill Street, Willington, Wallsend.

St. Paul the Apostle, Willington Quay
Consecrated in 1876

Originally the parish of Howdon Panns and before that part of the parish of St. Peter, Wallsend, it was founded in 1859. The nave was built in 1876, the chancel added in 1924 with pews, chancel screen, choir stalls and oak panelled sanctuary. In 1977 the church was re-ordered; with the screen moved to the rear of the church and a new altar set up in the chancel; the pews being replaced with chairs. Since 1976 the parish has been part of the Willington Team Ministry and is known as St. Paul, Willington Quay.

Times of Sunday Services:
9.30 a.m. Holy Eucharist
6.00 p.m. Evening Prayer (3 p.m. Evening Prayer (3 p.m. Oct to Easter)
Telephone: Vicarage – 0632 623574
Road Location: $\frac{1}{4}$ mile from the Tyne Tunnel, right turn off A187 Wallsend road at Campbells and Isherwood Ltd.

Church of the Good Shepherd, Wallsend
Planned for 1982/83

A Christian presence first appeared in this new housing area eleven years ago when a group of Methodists started a Sunday School and regular evening worship in a local school. Anglican services began in 1972, and when the Community Centre opened in 1973 both congregations moved into it. Over the years the two congregations have moved closer together holding regular joint services and this has been further enhanced by the scheme to build a shared church which not only involves the Methodists and Anglicans but also the United Reformed Church. It is hoped that the new church will be opened in Centennial year, and that many groups both secular and Christian will use it.

Times of Sunday Services:
　9.30 a.m. Holy Communion
10.30 a.m. Sunday School
　6.00 p.m. Evening Worship
Telephone: Vicarage – 627518
Road Location: Berwick Drive, Battle Hill.

Barratt
building
houses
to make
homes
in.

Barratt Newcastle Ltd.,
Barratt House, Airport Industrial Estate, Kenton,
Newcastle upon Tyne NE3 2EQ.
Telephone: Newcastle (0632) 869866.

St. Mary, Lesbury.

Saint Peter and Saint Paul, Lonhoughton.

ᴀLNWICK ᴅEANERY

St. John the Divine, Acklington
Consecrated in 1861

A fine Victorian Gothic building with a plain exterior and an unexpectedly pleasing interior, set in a spacious churchyard with an attractive Lych Gate. Some good modern woodwork includes an altar and reredos and communion rails, given as memorials to various members of the Milburn family of Guyzance.

Times of Sunday Services:
10.30 a.m. The Parish Communion (ASB Rite A)
Telephone: Warkworth Vicarage — Alnwick 711217
Road Location: Acklington Village on B6345.

St. Michael and All Angels, Alnham
The church is said to be built on the site of an ancient Roman Camp, but very little is known of its history prior to the Reformation. Probably it was first built and maintained by the lord of the manor, but in the twelfth century it was given by William de Vescy to the monks of Alnwick Abbey who most likely rebuilt it in its present form. The Transitional Chancel Arch dates from that period, and, if you look at the outside of the north wall of the nave, you will see traces of an arcade, indicating that at one time there was a north aisle to the church.

Times of Sunday Services:
3.00 p.m. Holy Communion (3rd Sunday)
3.00 p.m. Evensong (5th Sunday)
and as indicated on notice board
Telephone: Alwinton Vicarage — Rothbury 50203
Road Location: West of A697 to Alwinton.

St. John the Baptist, Alnmouth
Consecrated on November 1876

Alnmouth Church is an excellent specimen of an ecclesiastical building for a small village and it was built in 1874-1876 in the Early English style of Gothic architecture. It has a tower and spire at the west end and a south transept was added after the completion of construction of the main building which is of sandstone. It has a church clock with five bells and also a single tolling bell. The church has a capacity of about 200 people.

Times of Sunday Services:
8.00 a.m. Holy Communion (2nd and 4th Sundays)
9.30 a.m. Family Communion with sermon every Sunday
6.00 p.m. Evensong (1st, 3rd and 5th Sundays)
Telephone: Vicarage – Alnmouth 281
Road Location: On the east side of the main street in the centre of the village.

St. Michael's Church, Alnwick

Few traces remain of the church which existed before 1147 when Alnwick Abbey was founded. The present church dates from c.1380; a charter of Henry VI indicates considerable restoration in 1464 which made it one of the finest examples in the North of the Perpendicular style. Reordering by Adam brothers in 1782 produced a very ornate interior; restoration by Salvin in 1863 returned it to a style believed to be more in keeping with its origin. Among many interesting features, the spacious chancel which provided sittings for the 22 Canons of the Abbey is particularly noteworthy.

Times of Sunday Services:
 8.00 a.m. Holy Communion
 9.30 a.m. Parish Communion
11.15 a.m. Mattins (said) (1st and 3rd Sundays)
 6.00 p.m. Evensong
Telephone: Vicarage – Alnwick 602184
Road Location: A1/B6346, Canongate.

St. Michael and All Angels Church
Alwinton

Originally a Norman Church, numerous substantial alterations have been effected over the intervening 900 years; the last restoration being made in 1851. A curious feature in the plan of Alwinton Church is the great height of the chancel floor above the nave due to the steep slope on which the church is built, and because the chancel surmounts a Norman crypt, later used as a burial vault.

Times of Sunday Services:
9.30 a.m. Holy Communion
Telephone: Vicarage – Rothbury 50203
Road Location: Ordnance Survey 1:50,000 Sheet 80 Ref. 924058, or minor road off B6341 Elsdon to Rothbury.

St. Cuthbert, Amble
Consecrated on St. Luke's Day, 18 October 1870

Amble Parish was formed out of Warkworth Parish in 1869. It consists of the township of Amble, Gloster Hill and Coquet Island. The church was consecrated in 1870 having been built from designs by Messrs Austin and Johnson of Newcastle and is early Decorated in style. The organ was installed in 1876 and the east window dedicated in 1928. A choir vestry was added in 1929. The west window depicting events in the life of St. Cuthbert was commissioned for the Centenary in 1970.

Times of Sunday Services:
8.00 a.m. Holy Communion
9.30 a.m. Family Communion
6.00 p.m. Evening Prayer
Telephone: Vicarage — Alnwick 710273
Road Location: Church Street, Amble.

Bolton Chapel
Bolton
Consecrated in 13th century

A chapel of ease in the Parish of Edlingham. Although there has been considerable nineteenth century restoration, the foundation is ancient, and some Norman work survives. The chapel is mentioned in 1230, and was probably in the care of the Brethren of a Leper Hospital which was founded to the north of Bolton in 1227 under the terms of a licence granted by Prior of Durham who held the advowson until the Dissolution.

Times of Sunday Services:
11.15 a.m. Holy Communion
Telephone: Vicarage — Alnwick 602184
Road Location: A697 (near).

St. Andrew's Church, Boulmer

Chapel of ease to Longhoughton Parish Church.

The building in Boulmer Village erected by the Duke of Northumberland as a church and schoolroom in 1881.

The building is plain and functional and is used solely as the church now.

Times of Sunday Services:
8.00 a.m. Holy Communion (1st Sunday in month)
5.00 p.m. Holy Communion (remaining Sundays)
5.00 p.m. Evensong (1st Sunday)
Telephone: Longhoughton Vicarage — Longhoughton 664
Road Location: In Boulmer Village — Alnmouth to Boulmer Road.

St. Peter and St. Paul, Brinkburn Priory

Brinkburn Priory founded for Augustinian Canons by William Bertram I of Mitford about 1135. After the dissolution the priory passed into lay hands and a house was established on its site. The church remained in use but began to decay and regular services lapsed in 1683, although burials continued. Restoration was carried out in 1857 for the Cadogan family by Newcastle architect, Thomas Austin. After the house ceased to be occupied and the church again became disused it was placed in the guardianship of the State. The whole building is a superb example of the transition to northern Early Gothic architecture.

Times of Services:
7.30 p.m. Holy Communion on Ascension Day
other services from time to time
Telephone: Department of the Environment – Longframlington 628
Vicarage – Longframlington 200
Road Location: To be reached from the branch road between Weldon Bridge and Pauperhaugh, between Morpeth and Rothbury.

St. John the Divine, Chevington

The nave was built in 1858 and together with those of Acklington and Amble, 'born' from the Mother Church of St. Lawrence, Warkworth. The building consisting mainly of black dolomite whinstone taken from a local quarry, cost £1,200 of which sum Henry Earl Grey contributed £1,100 and Mr. Addison John Baker Esq of Cresswell gave £100. Earl Grey also gave the site and surrounding burial ground which has been closed for fifty years. The chancel and choir vestry were added in 1893 at a cost of £658 raised mainly by public subscription (the builder R. Gordon of Sunderland). There is a fine two manual organ, built by Harrison and Harrison of Durham. A new altar rail, clergy and choir stalls, done in light oak, together with a flat roof choir vestry, were added in 1958 to celebrate the Centenary. New lighting and complete rewiring was carried out by NEEB in 1980. The church accommodates 300.

Times of Sunday Services:
Last Sunday of Month: 9.30 a.m. Sung Mattins
6.00 p.m. Holy Communion
Other Sundays: 9.30 a.m. Family Communion
6.00 p.m. Sung Evensong
Telephone: Vicarage – Red Row 760 273
Road Location: A1068 Ashington to Alnwick via Amble and Warkworth.

St. Peter the Fisherman, Craster

In 1877 Thomas Wood Craster built a small stone mission in the village which bore his name in order that villagers need not make the 7 mile round trip to Embleton to attend Worship.

Built of local stone the little church tones in well with its background in this rugged Northumberland fishing village and it is greatly loved by many people who worship in it.

In 1977 the Centenary was celebrated and the Bishop of Newcastle dedicated the church giving it the name of 'St. Peter the Fisherman'.

Times of Sunday Services:
9.00 a.m. The Family Communion
Telephone: Vicarage – Embleton 660
Road Location: Take road 1340 out of Alnwick and follow sign posts.

St. John the Baptist, Edlingham
Consecrated in 1050

There may have been a church here in 740, which was replaced by another c.840. The first stone church dates from c.1050, and parts of this may have survived in the west wall. The main part of the present building is twelfth century. The fourteenth century tower was probably used for defence, and also as a 'lock up'. Interesting excavations are in progress at the adjacent Edlingham Castle, the fourteenth century owner of which, Sir William de Felton is buried within the church.

Times of Sunday Services:
Holy Communion on 2nd and 4th Sundays
8.00 a.m. Summer – 9.00 a.m. Winter
Telephone: Vicarage – Alnwick 602184
Road Location: B6341.

The Holy Trinity, Embleton Village

Dates from the early thirteenth century at which time the Barony was given to Simon de Montford in exchange for other lands. Later in the same century the patronage of the Living was given to Merton College, Oxford. Over the years many alterations have been made to the church culminating in the re-roofing of the nave and a new chancel being built in the middle of the last century.

In 1975 the old Vicarage which consisted of a fine example of a Vicar's Pele was sold and replaced. The old house still stands beside the church as a reminder of the days when the Border Counties were less peaceful than they are today. Visitors should notice the 'double Piscina' rather unimaginatively let into the wall of the old vestry by the Victorians. Also connections of the church with families of note, particularly the Crasters, Greys and Mandel-Creightons.

Times of Sunday Services:
10.00 a.m. The Family Communion
11.00 a.m. Mattins
Telephone: Vicarage – Embleton 660
Road Location: Take road 1340 from Alnwick and follow local sign posts.

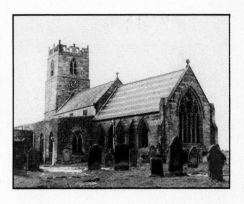

St. Michael and All Angels, Felton
Consecrated in 1199

William Bertram II the grandson of William Bertram I who founded Brinkburn Priory gave the church of Felton 'to Almighty God, St. Peter, and the Canons of Brinkburn' shortly before his death in AD 1199. The structure of the church is chiefly of two dates. It consists of a chancel and nave with north and south aisles and a south porch. The earlier work is to be seen in the chancel and nave the later having originally been without aisles. The aisles were added in the fourteenth century. Points to note: the east window in the south aisle worked in a single 6 feet 6 inches by 4 feet stone, probably inserted in AD 1331. Also the fourteenth century effigy of a priest in the north aisle on the floor.

Times of Sunday Services:
8.00 a.m. and 9.30 a.m.
Telephone: Vicarage – Felton 263
Road Location: Turn west immediately on the north side of Felton bridge up the hill on road number U3048.

St. Peter's Church, Glanton
Built in 1891

A daughter church of St. Bartholomew's, Whittingham.

St. Peter's is a wooden structure, originally built as a Mission Room and Sunday School in 1891. It was licensed for Divine Service and the celebration of the holy sacraments by the Bishop of Newcastle on 12 April 1922.
Times of Sunday Services:
9.15 a.m. Holy Communion (1st, 3rd and 5th Sundays of month)
Telephone: Vicarage – Whittingham 224
Road Location: Front Street, Glanton.

Christ Church, Hepple
Consecrated in 1893

Christ Church, Hepple, was founded by Sir Walter Buchanan-Riddell as a chapel of ease to Rothbury Parish, and consecrated on 10 July 1893 by the Rt. Rev. Ernest Wilberforce, Bishop of Newcastle. The architect, Mr. C. Hodgson Fowler, adopted a simple late perpendicular style, using local stone. The interior is distinguished by an Italianate Altar piece, with a copy of Perugino's painting of the Crucifixion at Florence. The font bowl is possibly of Saxon origin, and was brought from Kirkfield, West Hepple, the site of a former church.
Time of Sunday Service:
9.00 a.m. Holy Communion (alternate Sundays)
Telephone: Vicarage – Rothbury 20482
Road Location: B6341, 5 miles west of Rothbury.

St. Mary the Virgin, Holystone

Holystone Church was rebuilt in 1848. Evidence suggests a Norman church stood on this site, rebuilding and repair occurring frequently over the past 900 years. Holystone is an important site in the early Christian history of Northumberland. St. Mungo's well on the south side of the village is reputed to be one of S. Kentigern's places of preaching and baptism. St. Paulinus baptized at St. Ninians well in 627 (later known as St. Paulinus's or the Lady's well).
Time of Sunday Service:
11.00 a.m. Holy Communion
Telephone: Vicarage – Rothbury 50203
Road Location: Minor road off B6341 Elsdon to Rothbury.

St. Michael and All Angels, Howick
Church founded late Saxon era.

Totally rebuilt in the eighteenth century by Sir Henry Grey on Classical style and restored and enlarged in the nineteenth century by the 3rd Earl Grey in the Neo Norman style.

Parish church as well as chapel to Grey family of Howick Hall. Distinguished family in public service. Probably most outstanding member of the family was Charles 2nd Earl Grey, who served as Prime Minister in 1832 and moved the Reform Bill of 1832. His tomb lies in the church.

Times of Sunday Services:
10.30 a.m. Parish Communion
Telephone: Longhoughton Vicarage — Longhoughton 664
Road Location: In the grounds of Howick Hall. Longhoughton to Craster road.

St. Mary, Lesbury
12th century origins – original building probably dates from early in the 12th century

A typical ancient village church, thought to have been built on the site of an original Saxon church of which however no trace remains. The present building is of Norman origin and it can be said with reasonable certainty that it was built in its original form in the early part of the twelfth century. However owing to many alterations and repairs carried out over the centuries little of the original structure remains. Mid-nineteenth century major repairs give the south aspect of the church a very Victorian appearance.

Times of Sunday Services:
8.00 a.m. Holy Communion (1st, 3rd and 5th Sundays)
11.00 a.m. Family Communion with sermon every Sunday
6.00 p.m. Evensong (2nd and 4th Sundays)
Telephone: Vicarage — Alnmouth 281
Road Location: Close to main road east-west through village.

St Mary's Church, Longframlington.

St. Mary the Virgin, Longframlington
The church dates from the late twelfth century and until 1891 was a chapel of ease to Felton; since that date Longframlington has been an independent parish. The church was carefully restored in the late nineteenth century retaining its fine Norman chancel arch.

Times of Sunday Services:
9.30 a.m. Holy Communion
6.00 p.m. Evensong
Telephone: Vicarage — Longframlington 200
Road Location: At the junction of the Morpeth-Wooler road A697 with the branch road to Rothbury in Longframlington.

St. Peter and St. Paul, Longhoughton
Consecrated in Saxon era

Remaining features of original church are Saxon chancel arch and piers of tower arch. Church rebuilt in 1080 with strong defensive tower (used for defence until seventeenth century). Enlarged in twelfth century with south aisle, and successfully restored in 1874.

Main features lie in the Saxon arches, early Norman tower, and transitional aisle and window. Also a mediaeval squint.

Previous vicars included George Duncan (1696-1730) who added revealing comments on the characters of his parishioners in the pages of the registers. During the seventeenth and eighteenth centuries the Church and Vicarage were reputed to act as the distribution centre for smugglers from Boulmer.

The church also serves as station church to RAF Boulmer.

Times of Sunday Services:
9.00 a.m. Parish Communion
6.30 p.m. Evensong (3.00 p.m. in winter)
Telephone: Vicarage – Longhoughton 664
Road Location: Alnwick to Howick and Craster.

Mission Church, Newton by the Sea

Another Mission Church to Embleton. Newton Church was built about 1870 between the villages of High and Low Newton. Services are held in the church during the summer months. At other times of the year in houses.

Times of Sunday Services:
5.30 p.m. Sunday Evening (once a fortnight)
Telephone: Vicarage – Embleton 660
Road Location: Take road 1340 out of Alnwick and follow local sign posts.

All Saints, Rennington Village

Like Rock, Rennington Church was originally a chapel of Embleton. The old Norman church was replaced by a new building in 1831 which was enlarged in 1865.

The parish was united with Rock into a single united Benefice and the new Parish was united with Embleton in 1975. Thus was restored the original arrangement for the church in this area.

Times of Sunday Services: Once a fortnight (alternatively with Rock).
Telephone: Vicarage – Embleton 660,
Road Location: Take road 1340 from Alnwick and follow local signposts.

St. Philip and St. James, Rock Village

Originally part of the Parish of Embleton. A church dedicated to St. Philip and St. James was built about 1176.

During the seventeenth century the church building became ruinous and was rebuilt in 1806 at the expense of Charles Bosanquet. Further improvements were made in 1855. In 1866 an aisle was added on the north side to house a large Cathedral size organ, the gift of Mr. Holford Bosanquet who designed it and caused it to be built by the London organ builders of Grey and Davison. (Originally the instrument was powered by an engine which ran on petroleum gas.)

Features to notice are the Norman door to the church and the place where the rood screen originally fitted into the chancel arch where can still be seen crude cuts of a mediaeval stone mason which represent the Holy Spirit in the form of a bird.

Times of Sunday Services:
Once a fortnight (alternating with Rennington)
Telephone: Vicarage – Embleton 660
Road Location: Take road 1340 from Alnwick and follow local signposts.

All Saints, Rothbury

The fragment of the Saxon Cross of Rothbury, which now serves as pedestal to the font, indicates that a Christian church has stood on this site for nearly 1200 years. The carving of the Ascension of our Lord, on its north side, is said to be the oldest of its kind in Britain. (c.800AD). The chancel of the present church is thirteenth century, but the nave and tower were rebuilt in 1850. The pulpit, screen, and other fine wood carvings were gifts of the Lords Armstrong of Cragside.

Times of Sunday Services:
8.00 a.m. Holy Communion
10.00 a.m. Parish Communion
6.30 p.m. Evensong
Telephone: Vicarage – Rothbury 20482
Road Location: Church Street, Rothbury.

St. James' Church, Shilbottle
Consecrated in 1885

The church, designed by W. S. Hicks in the Late Decorated Style, stands on the site of former Norman and Saxon churches. Some features of the Norman church have been retained including the porch doorway and chancel archway and the font. The tower, simple but massive, forms a landmark for miles around. The stained glass east window is the village memorial placed there in 1921. A small window in the south transept is by the well-known stained glass artist, Kemp. The church includes some richly carved screens and panelling and a beautiful chancel roof decorated with symbols of the Passion.

Times of Sunday Services:
9.30 a.m. Parish Eucharist
6.00 p.m. Evening Prayer
Telephone: Vicarage – Shilbottle 247
Road Location: Middle Road, Shilbottle.

St. Andrew's Church, Thropton
Dedicated in 1902

St. Andrew's, Thropton, in the parish of Rothbury, was built by public subscription in 1902 on land donated by Lord Armstrong of Cragside and dedicated for public worship. Its rough-cast white-washed walls are prominent as you leave the village on the Cartington Road. The pews were brought from St. Barnasbas, Thorneyford, Kirkley, in the parish of Ponteland, in 1973.
Times of Sunday Services:
9.00 a.m. Holy Communion (alternate Sundays)
Telephone: Vicarage – Rothbury 20482
Road Location: B6341 2 miles west of Rothbury.

St. Lawrence's Church, Warkworth
Consecrated probably early 7th century

An outstanding Norman church, built on Saxon foundations. The original church was probably a foundation of Saints Aidan and Oswald, and may have housed relics of St. Lawrence, sent by Pope Vitalian to Oswald's successor, King Oswin. The church was seized by forces loyal to the Old Pretender in 1715 and prayers were offered for him as King James III by the Rebel's chaplain, following which the Pretender was proclaimed King at the Market Cross.

Recent incumbents include Richard Watson Dixon, a distinguished church historian and poet.
Times of Sunday Services:
9.00 a.m. The Parish Communion (ASB Rite A)
8.00 a.m. Holy Communion (2nd Sunday – ASB Rite B)
Telephone: Vicarage – Alnwick 711217
Road Location: Dial Place, Warkworth.

St. Bartholomew's Church, Whittingham

Numerous alterations and additions have resulted in a variety of architectural styles from the eighth to twentieth centuries. The lower parts of the west wall and tower probably date from c.737; the masonry immediately above is later Saxon and the upper section of the tower was rebuilt in 1839-40. There was formerly a chapel in the south transept dedicated to St. Peter, of which only an Early English piscina remains. A ground plan of the church is displayed dating other parts of the building and notes on its history are available.
Times of Sunday Services:
11.00 a.m. Holy Communion (1st Sunday)
Other Sundays: 8.00 a.m. Holy Communion
          11.00 a.m. Mattins
Telephone: Whittingham 224
Road Location: On road in Whittingham signposted for Eslington and Netherton.

ALNWICK CASTLE
ALNWICK, NORTHUMBERLAND

Admission

Adults	£1.00
Children under 16 ..	50p

Special Rates for organised parties:

Adults	80p
Children under 16 ..	40p

1982
OPEN TO THE PUBLIC
16th MAY to 8th OCTOBER
Daily, except SATURDAYS

1 p.m. to 5 p.m.
(No Admission after 4.30 p.m.)

(HOME OF THE DUKE OF NORTHUMBERLAND).

This magnificent border fortress dates back to the 11th Century, when the earliest parts of the present castle were erected by Yvo de Vescy, the first Norman Baron of Alnwick, who became the owner of the town soon after 1096. The Percy family who had accompanied William the Conqueror in 1066, came into ownership in 1309. The main restoration work bringing the castle to its present appearance, was carried out by the 4th Duke between 1854 and 1865.

The rugged medieval exterior belies the richness of the interior, decorated in the classical style of the Italian Renaissance: this replaced the Gothic decoration carried out by Robert Adam in the eighteenth century.

The principal apartments including the Armoury, Guard Chamber and Library are on view, also the Dungeon, State Coach and Museum of early British and Roman Relics.

There are pictures by Titian, Canaletto, Van Dyck and other famous artists, together with fine furniture, Meissen China and various historical heirlooms.

The landscape to the North, over the River Aln, was laid out by Capability Brown, and can be enjoyed from the terrace of the castle.

Free Parking outside the Castle

Enquiries to: The Supervisor, Estates Office, Alnwick Castle
(Tel: Alnwick 602722 or Alnwick 602207)

(Admission to the Regimental Museum of The Royal Northumberland Fusiliers, within the Castle Grounds, is subject to a separate charge of 20p – children 10p).

NO CONDUCTED TOURS UNLESS REQUESTED

Saint Mary's Church, Belford.

BAMBURGH & GLENDALE DEANERY

St. Aidan's Church, Bamburgh
Consecrated: 13th century

St. Aidan's is one of the three finest parish churches in Northumberland (others are Alnwick and Norham). Origins date from AD 635 when St. Aidan came to Lindisfarne from Iona. Present building is thirteenth century. Chancel, said to be second longest in the country (60 ft), contains magnificent historical reredos in Caen stone. There is an effigy of Grace Darling in the North Aisle. Her memorial is so sited in the churchyard that it can be seen from passing ships. Ancient crypt discovered in 1837.

Times of Sunday Services:
9.30 a.m. The Eucharist
4.00 p.m. Evensong (October-May)
6.00 p.m. Evensong (June-September)
Telephone: Vicarage — Bamburgh (066-84) 295
Road Location: Church Street, Bamburgh.

St. Ebba's Church, Beadnell
Consecrated: Present building 1746, rebuilt 1860

Ruins of a 13C Chapel of St. Ebba can be seen at Ebb's Nook near the harbour and ealier chapels are said to have stood on the same spot. The present church replaced one on a nearby site and is a simple but attractive village church. Before 1854 when the parish of Beadnell was constituted, St. Ebba's was a chapel of ease to St. Aidan's, the mother church at Bamburgh. St. Ebba, the sister of St. Oswald, was Abbess of Coldingham. A fine modern war-memorial window in the church recalls their liberality to the church, and depicts other Northern saints. Local skill and craftsmanship have also produced attractive kneelers.

Times of Sunday Services:
9.15 a.m. Sung Eucharist
6.00 p.m. Evensong and Address
Telephone: Vicarage — Seahouses 720223
Road Location: At the north end of Beadnell Village, just off the B1340 Alnwick-Bamburgh Road.

St. Mary's Church, Belford

The first stone church was built in Norman times about 1200. In 1615 the church was entirely rebuilt as a plain rectangular design with a door at the west end of the south side and a bell turret. Originally the east end was a private chapel for Belford Hall and adjoined the church. Extensively renovated in 1700. Restoration of the chancel by J. Dobson started in 1828, and the following year the church as we see it now was built.

Features to note: clock in tower, show case beside pulpit containing names of fallen in Great War and 1939-45 War, the gallery over the side aisle, greatly used as a meeting place for organisations in the village, the vault under the vestry discovered in 1966.

Times of Sunday Services:
9.00 a.m. Holy Communion
6.00 p.m. Evensong (some Sundays)
Telephone: Vicarage — Belford 545
Road Location: A1 until further notice — construction of by-pass in progress.

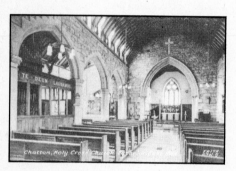

Holy Cross Church, Chatton

The original church at Chatton was granted to Alnwick Abbey between 1157-1184 by William de Vesci. After the dissolution of the monasteries the patronage was vested in the Earldom of Percy. Sadly in 1713 the Norman Church was destroyed by fire, and the present building then constructed near the original site.

The organ situated on the north side of the church was built by Holdich of London and formerly housed in Magdalen College, Oxford.

Times of Sunday Services:
9.00 a.m. Holy Communion (2nd, 4th and 5th Sundays of month)
10.30 a.m. URC United Service (1st Sunday of month)
6.00 p.m. Evening Prayer (3rd Sunday of month)
Telephone: Vicarage — Wooler 81468
Road Location: Five miles east of Wooler on the B6348.

St. Peter's Church, Chillingham

St. Peter's occupies the site of a twelfth century church. The interior has the splendid combination of the old and new. As well as ancient stonework, the church retains its nineteenth century box pews whilst the sanctuary was completely modernised in 1967. In the south chapel is the famous fifteenth century tomb of Sir Ralph de Grey.

Times of Sunday Services:
12.00 noon Holy Communion (1st and 5th Sundays of month)
Telephone: Vicarage — Wooler 81468
Road Location: The village lies 1 mile south of Chatton which is on the B6348. Travel down the bank opposite Chillingham Post Office, crossing the ford and the church is on the hillside at the end of the road.

St. Mary and St. Michael's Church
Doddington

Built of the site of a twelfth century church, the present building has undergone various alterations. The most prominent being the reversal of the interior, resulting in the chancel being at the west end and the baptistry at the east.

Two grave steels can be seen in the porch and a monument in the sanctuary is in the memory of Horace St. Paul, Count of the Holy Roman Empire.

In the south-eastern corner of the churchyard is a watchhouse, built in 1826, when there was alarm about bodysnatchers operating on behalf of Scottish surgeons.

Times of Sunday Services:
9.00 a.m. (1st and 3rd Sundays of month)
11.15 a.m. Mattins (2nd and 4th Sunday of month)
Telephone: Vicarage — Wooler 81468
Road Location: The village lies 2¼ miles north of Wooler on the A6111.

St. Maurice's Church, Eglingham

The church is probably of Saxon foundation. King Coelwulf granted Eglingham to Lindisfarne Priory in 738. The chancel arch may date from this period. The chancel and tower are Early English. 'Ogle Pew' the transept on north side is built over Ogle vault: The Collingwood vault is below the chancel. The font dates from 1663. The tower was a refuge for village females in times of Border raids — note window in wall between tower and nave for viewing services.

Times of Sunday Services:
8.00 a.m. Holy Communion most Sundays (series II)
11.00 a.m. Mattins alternate Sundays (series II)
3.30 or 6.00 p.m. Evensong alternate Sundays (series II)
10.15 a.m. First Sunday in month the parish communion
Telephone: Vicarage — Powburn 382
Road Location: B6346 — 7 miles NW of Alnwick (OS grid 106195).

St. Maurice, Ellingham

Year of Consecration: Present church built 1862, previous churches on the same site going back to 1150, possibly even earlier.

Some parts of the Norman church incorporated in the present building: piscina, font bowl, some pieces of window tracery. Memorial tablets and windows, especially to the Haggerston and Baker Cresswell families, and to former incumbents. A list of former incumbents dates back to 1150. Interesting light fittings and a locally-carved font cover are also worth seeing, and St. Maurice's Well, in the Glebe Field beside the wooden bridge.

St. Maurice was an officer of the Roman Theban Legion during the reign of Diocletian. He and his companions were martyred in the third century in Switzerland for refusing pagan sacrifices and refusing to attack the innocent.

Time of Sunday Service:
10.45 a.m. Sung Eucharist
Telephone: Vicarage — Seahouses 720223
Road Location: On the outskirts of Ellingham Village, lying 1 mile to the east of the A1, 7½ miles north of Alnwick.

St. Michael's Church, Ilderton, Alnwick
Year of Consecration before 1121

Long narrow modern nave suggests pre-Conquest foundations. Only parts of tower and tower arch date to thirteenth century. Largely rebuilt in eighteenth century. It possesses, now in a museum, a chalice dated 1583, the only piece of Newcastle Silver from Elizabethan times. The church has little history because until the mid-eighteenth century it and the parish were so frequently pillaged.

Times of Sunday Services:
9.00 a.m. Holy Communion (series III/ASB)
(except 3rd Sunday in month)
1st Sunday Mattins 1662
Telephone: Vicarage – Wooler 81551
Road Location: A697 – 24 miles north of Morpeth, turn left, 1 mile turn left, church on left (OS grid 018219).

St. Michael and All Angels Church, Ingram

Notable for its quiet peaceful setting, on the South Bank of the Breamish, opposite the former Church School, now a National Park Information Centre. A Saxon foundation, with an early Norman tower added, it reached its greatest extent in mid-fourteenth century – with north and south chantry chapels, wide north and south aisles and a long chancel. By the mid-nineteenth century this glory had long departed. A fine restoration was completed in 1879, The Rector, the Rev. James Allgood effecting this as a memorial to his wife and two sons who had been killed in a railway accident. The tower was taken down and rebuilt in 1905.

Note: Font, Priest's memorial and sun dial.

Times of Sunday Services:
1st and 3rd Sundays – Holy Communion 11.30 a.m. (ASB)
2nd, 4th and 5th Sundays – Evensong 6.00 p.m. (ASB)
Telephone: Vicarage – Wooler 81427
Road Location: 3 miles west leaving A697, ½ a mile north of Powburn.

St. Gregory the Great, Kirknewton

A place of Christian worship has stood here since the eleventh century or earlier. The chancel and south transept known as the Burrell chapel both date from the latter part of the fifteenth century built probably from the stones of the ruined Norman church. The church in its present form is the result of a restoration by John Dobson of Newcastle completed in 1860 with the tower being added some years later. The great treasure of the church is the stone relief of the Adoration of the Magi set in the wall to the north of the chancel arch. Note also the carved wooden relief of the Nativity and the modern memorial window.

Times of Sunday Services:
10.30 a.m. every Sunday
1st, 3rd and 5th – The Parish Communion
2nd and 4th – Morning Prayer
Telephone: Vicarage – Milfield 219
Road Location: B6351 Akeld to Yetholm. A697 Wooler/Coldstream to Akeld (2 miles). B6351 Akeld/Yeavering/Kirknewton (2½ miles).

St. Hilda's Church, Lucker
Dedicated in 1874
The church was built to replace the former one which was destroyed by fire. The whole cost was met by the Duke of Northumberland.

The oak choirstalls and pulpit were carved by a team of local men in 1904. Each has carved his initials on the back of the panel he worked.
Times of Sunday Services:
11.00 a.m. Holy Communion
Telephone: Vicarage – Bamburgh 295
Road Location: B1341 – Adderstone to Bamburgh.

St. Paul's Church, North Sunderland
Consecrated in January 1834
Built in 1833, to serve the township of North Sunderland, which was part of the parish of Bamburgh – it became the parish church in 1834.

The site was formerly that of an ancient Pele Tower. The remains of which were removed to accommodate the new building.

Designed by Anthony Salvin – the Duke of Northumberland's architect, it is an apsidal church of Norman style with single aisle and set in a now closed graveyard.
Times of Sunday Services:
10.00 a.m. Family Communion
6.30 p.m. Evensong
Telephone: Vicarage – 0665 720202
Road Location: Main Street, North Sunderland.

Holy Trinity Church, Old Bewick
Ancient – restored in 19th century
In 1107 Queen Maud gave the Manor of Old Bewick to Tynemouth Priory in memory of her father, slain at Alnwick and buried at Tynemouth. The Norman Arch of the sanctuary and windows date from that period. The fourteenth century effigy in the choir is said to have been much damaged by Lesley's troops in 1640. By eighteenth century it was almost a total ruin. Restored in 1867.
Times of Sunday Services:
9.30 a.m. Holy Communion (series II)
(Not 1st Sunday, when Parish Communion is at Eglingham, nor 5th Sunday)
Telephone: Vicarage – Powburn 382
Road Location: B6346 $8\frac{1}{2}$ miles NW Alnwick bear right for Charlton, 1 mile turn right for church (OS grid 068221).

St. James' Church, South Charlton
Consecrated in 1862 (12 September)

There was a chapel in the village in the mid thirteenth century which was still used as late as 1750 but afterwards fell into ruin. Until 1860 it was part of Ellingham parish but the relationship was such that the parishoners of South Charlton had to be ordered to attend the parish church. Now part of the Glendale group of parishes served by the team clergy.

Times of Sunday Services:
Odd Sundays in month 9.15 a.m. – HC ASB
Even Sundays in month 11.00 a.m. – HC ASB
One Sunday in month (4th) 1662
One Sunday in month (3rd) 1662 Mattins
Telephone: as for Eglingham – Powburn 382
Road Location: A1 – from Alnwick 6 miles north turn left onto B6347, 1 mile church on left.

St. Mary's Church, Wooler
Ancient Foundation

The church was severely damaged by fire in 1762 and 1763. It was rebuilt in 1765 and extended in 1826, so that only the tower and south aisle remain of the original church. In 1913 chancel and clergy vestry were added; in 1922 gallery removed. The east window and two chancel windows, all modern, are the most striking feature and a valuable aid to worship and teaching. The only memorials in the church are to William Haigh who exercised a vigorous ministry of building and renewal from 1805-1835.

Times of Sunday Services:
  8.00 a.m. Holy Communion (series III ASB)
10.00 a.m. Sung Eucharist (series III ASB)
  6.00 p.m. Evensong alternating with evening service in UR church
Telephone: Vicarage – Wooler 81551
Road Location: A697 26 miles north of Morpeth (OS grid 993280).

Fun indoors

Blyth Sports Centre

Concordia

Cafeteria

Childrens Activities

Swimming

Leisure Pool

Indoor Sports

Bar & Cafeteria

Squash

Bowls

Childrens Events

Indoor Sports

Luxury Sauna

Squash

Free Parking

Special Events

Bar

Solarium

Blyth Sports Centre

Tel Blyth 2581 2943
Signposted from
Blyth Town Centre.
Free Parking
Open
7 days a week

Concordia

Tel Cramlington
717421
Cramlington Town Centre
SE. Northumberland.
Free Parking
Open
7 days a week

St. Andrew's Church, Bothal Village

ᴍORPETH ᴅEANERY

Holy Sepulchre Church, Ashington

In March 1885 at a meeting of parishioners called by the Hon. and Rev. W. E. Ellis, Rector of Bothal, held in the Ashington School, a scheme for erecting a church and forming a new parish was introduced and explained. The Duke of Portland promised a donation of £500 towards the undertaking, and also a free gift of two acres of land for the site of the Church and burial land. The Ashington Coal Company also promised £300, making a total of £800 towards the cost.

It was estimated that the cost of the project would be £1,100 to £1,200.

The church was built by William Carse and Sons of Amble. The first baptism was administered on Sunday 6 February 1887. The church was opened for service under licence from the Bishop on 30 January 1887.

There had been arrangements to have a bell tower when the church was first designed, but the Coal Company objected because it would keep their employees awake when they were not down the pit.

There is no record kept of how many Vicars there have been in the Parish but none could have been here longer than Rev. (Sammy) Davison, from 1905 to 1943.

Times of Sunday Services:
9.00 a.m. Sung Eucharist – 3.30 p.m. Evensong
Telephone: Vicarage – Ashington 813358
Road Location: Central.

St. Andrew's Church, Bolam

A once-thriving village has gone, a Country Park has come, but Bolam St. Andrew remains – a gem of a church on a gem of a site; a place of peace and inspiration for many, full of intriguing questions for the antiquarian. Noted for its late Saxon tower, tall and unbuttressed; its Norman moulded chancel arch and the later porch arch; the Short-flatt Chapel with its stone effigy of Robert de Reymes, a Border knight, etc. Church and churchyard bear witness to generations of the Middleton family of Belsay and successive owners of Shortflatt Tower: several fine eighteenth century headstones may also be found.

Times of Sunday Services:
8.00 a.m. Holy Communion (1st, 3rd and 5th Sundays)
11.00 a.m. Parish Communion (2nd and 4th Sundays)
Mattins (3rd and 5th Sundays); Family Service (1st Sunday)
Telephone: Rectory – Whalton (067 075) 360
Road Location: Off minor road from Bolam Country Park to Whalton.

St. Andrew's Church, Bothal Village

Within a bow shot from Bothal Castle stands St. Andrew's Church, built possibly about 882. Enlarged in Norman times by the first Bertram about 1150. Features: alabaster tomb of Ralph 3rd Lord Ogle, Norman Piscina, Jacobean altar rails, Elizabethan communion cup dated 1571, bell turret and thirteenth century glass in windows.

Times of Sunday Services:
11.00 a.m. Parish Communion
 6.00 p.m. Evensong (1st Sunday of Month — March-December)
Telephone: Vicarage — Morpeth 56292
Road Location: 1 mile south off A197 Morpeth-Ashington road at Pegswood.

Holy Trinity, Cambo
Consecrated c. AD 1842

Present church built about AD 1842 by Sir John Trevelyan of Wallington Hall. Cambo originally a chapelry of Hartburn. The early chapel (twelfth-thirteenth centuries) was demolished in 1795, a few coffin covers preserved and now set into wall of present building, inside opposite main entrance. Silver cup made in the reign of Charles I was presented to Cambo Church by Sir John Trevelyan for use as a Chalice (not kept in present building). Sir Charles Trevelyan added tower with clock and bells. He also rebuilt present roof. Four windows added as family memorials and window in tower added by Sir Charles' widow. Major internal reconstruction of Cambo Church made in 1965, including removal of old panelling and pews installed.

Times of Sunday Services:
Vary monthly
Telephone: Vicarage — 0830 40260
Road Location: A696 Newcastle-Jedburgh road via Ponteland and Belsay.

St. Bartholomew, Apostle and Martyr
Cresswell Village
Consecrated in 1836

Originally a 'district church' within the ancient parish of Woodhorn, the present building was erected specifically to serve the spiritual needs of the Baker-Cresswell family and their estate workers.

The building is of neo-Norman design with nave, lower chancel and bell cote. Note the two east windows by Thomas Willement (1786-1871) each containing six medallions portraying major events in the earthly life of Our Lord from the Annunciation to the Ascension in a style of about 1200.

Two modern windows in the south wall of the sanctuary are memorials to members of the Baker-Cresswell family and show their gaily coloured coat of arms which includes sheaves of corn and squirrels.

Times of Sunday Services:
10.30 a.m. Parish Communion (Every Sunday)
 6.00 p.m. Evensong and Sermon (Last Sunday in month)
Telephone: as for Lynemouth
Road Location: Turn off A1068 at Ellington, follow Cresswell signs (1½ miles).

St. Andrew Hartburn Ancient Church, Hartburn
Consecrated early in 11th century

In 1207 King John confirmed Hartburn to Tynemouth Priory. In 1255 Henry III gave it to St. Alban's 'to provide the Monks and their Guests with a competent supply of bread and ale'. Skeletons in the tower, forensically dated pre-1100, suggest Waltheof as donor and Tynemouth Priory as builder. Two daggers above a Maltese Cross on the doorpost tell of a Knights Templar Preceptory here in 1250, and the Early English architecture speaks of little subsequent change. Of special interest are the Masons' marks, carved heads, fish, Napoleonic banners, Florentine lamps. The light, airiness of the building contributes to its frequent description – 'serenity', 'peacefulness'. The churchyard contains many fascinating memorial stones from 1693.
Times of Sunday Services:
9.00 a.m. The Communion
11.00 a.m. Communion and Mattins alternatively
Telephone: Vicarage – Hartburn 276
Road Location: At Hartburn on B6343.

St. Cuthbert's Church, Hebron

For a large part of its history, Hebron or Hebburn, was in the parish of Bothal. From 1683 it had its own resident clergyman at Priestbridge. In 1674 the church was in a ruinous state. Rebuilding took place in 1793. All that remains of the old church is the present chancel arch. An ancient chapel once existed at Causey Bridge, said to be one of the resting places of St. Cuthbert's body. No trace of this can be seen now.
Times of Sunday Services:
9.15 a.m. Holy Communion (2nd and 4th Sundays)
2.30 p.m. Holy Communion (1st Sunday)
2.30 p.m. Evensong (3rd and 5th Sundays)
Telephone: Vicarage – Morpeth 790253
Road Location: Three miles north of Morpeth and half a mile east of the A1.

St. Wilfrid, Kirkharle
Consecrated in 14th century

Nave and chancel, no tower or side aisles. West gable, porch and bell cope, added by Sir William Loraine in eighteenth century. Chancel windows filled with reticulated tracery. The design is one of simplicity and great beauty. Three sedilia in south wall of chancel; piscina with projecting basin close behind them. Priest's door in same wall. Remarkable and unusual feature in chancel – two low side windows in north and south walls – purpose unknown. Font fifteenth-sixteenth centuries was once in All Saints', Newcastle. Abandoned when old church of All Saints' destroyed and brought to Kirkharle about 1884 by Mr. George Anderson of Little Harle. The font on each of its eight sides a shield of arms of old Northumbrian families. Launcelot (Capability) Brown born at Kirkharle and baptised August 30th 1716. Educated at Cambo (present Village Hall) and first employed as gardener under Sir William Loraine.
Times of Services: Vary monthly
Telephone: Vicarage – 0830 40260
Road Location: A696 Newcastle-Jedburgh via Ponteland and Belsay, approximately 21 miles left at Hexham crossroads.

St. Bartholomew, Kirkheaton
Consecrated in 1753

The earliest known record of Kirkheaton is of Kyrke Heton Subsidy Roll in the list of possessions of Hexham Priory in AD 1296. 'Heton' means 'farm on the hill'. Originally, a detached chapelry of Chollerton, from Reformation times regarded as extra-parochial. The present church was built by Mrs. Dorothy Windsor. The chamfered base course and the north wall of nave appear to be mediaeval. It is thought that the four grotesque heads under the capping stones of the nave gables outside can claim to date from an earlier chapel. Chalice dated 1774 is by J. Young and Orlando Jackson. From his notebook, Fr. T. Harris (1865-1867) then chaplain to Kirkheaton Church, wrote, "29 Oct Evensong 6 p.m. A terribly stormy day, snow: chancel quite a pool – had a fire in the Vestry which filled the church with smoke – had to speak to the choir about spitting etc., in church'.

Times of Sunday Services: Vary monthly.
Telephone: Vicarage – Kirkwhelpington 40260
Road Location: A696 Newcastle road via Ponteland and Belsey. Kirkheaton shown on first signpost left after Belsay.

St. Bartholomew's Church, Kirkwhelpington
Consecrated in 13th century

Kirkwhelpington Parish Church thought to be cruciform at one time. The tower is low and broad, with heavy buttresses. Long nave with centre aisle only and renewed east end. A tower arch to the nave shows zigzag decoration, remains a mystery. Two fourteenth century bells are inscribed respectively, Ave Maria graciae plena and Ricardus Watson (a former Vicar). Plain sedilia double-pointed-trefoiled. The font is octagonal seventeenth century, resting on reversed capital of fourteenth century pier. Pulpit small, plain, mahogany, with tester, dated 1797. Large monument mid-eighteenth century inside church on north wall in memory of Gowen Aynsley and wife, Mary. Sir Charles Parsons (of turbine engine fame) and Lady Katharine buried here; memorial in church. The Revd. John Hodgson, Vicar (1823-1834) wrote his History of Northumberland in Kirkwhelpington Vicarage.

Times of Sunday Services: Vary monthly
Telephone: Vicarage – 0830 40260
Road Location: A696 Newcastle-Jedburgh road.

St. Aidan's Church, Linton
Rebuilt in circa 1965

Simple modern church hall comprising a church room and a kitchen/meeting room, serving the community of Linton of about 150 houses.

Times of Sunday Services:
10.15 a.m.
  6.30 p.m. Combined evening service with the Methodists
Telephone: Vicarage – Ashington 813358
Road Location: On the Ashington to Alnwick road, 2 miles out of Ashington.

St. John the Evangelist, Longhirst
Consecrated in 1876
The parish of Longhirst was formed in 1875. Before that date it was part of the parish of Bothal. The church was built in 1876 and the architect was Sir Arthur Blonfield. A tower with a spire is at the north-west corner of the building. The oak chancel screen was carved by parishioners and the Revd. R. Proctor, Vicar from 1885-1916.
Times of Sunday Services:
8.30 a.m. Holy Communion (1st and 5th Sundays)
9.15 a.m. Holy Communion (3rd Sunday)
10.30 a.m. Holy Communion (1st, 2nd and 4th Sundays)
10.30 a.m. Mattins (5th Sunday)
Telephone: Vicarage – Morpeth 790253
Road Location: At south end of village, on junction of B1337 and Pegswood Road.

St. Helen's Church, Longhorsley
Norman church, half a mile south of the village, it possibly replaced a wooden Saxon building. Earliest record of vicar, 1299. In 1783 the church was entirely rebuilt on the old foundations. It was a plain structure, the main feature being an attractive trefoil chancel arch. Lack of facilities and the need for extensive renovation, made it necessary to abandon it in 1966. The old Church of England school in the village was then taken over, adapted, and is now the church. It was built in 1848. In 1981, the porch on the old church, was dismantled and rebuilt on the west end and is now the main entrance. Other alterations and improvements are planned.
Times of Sunday Services:
9.30 a.m. Parish Communion
11.00 a.m. Mattins (1st Sunday)
11.00 a.m. Family Service (3rd Sunday)
Telephone: Vicarage – Longhorsley 218
Road Location: West road off A697.

St. Aidan's Church, Lynemouth
Consecrated in 1961
Lynemouth St. Aidan's conventional district under Woodhorn 1925-1961; church and hall until September 1959; after a hall being built in 1955. The church cum hall was made into a church in 1961. On 7 June 1961 the church was consecrated by the Rt. Revd. Hugh Ashdown, Lord Bishop of Newcastle and after 36 years as a conventional district Lynemouth became a parish.
Times of Sunday Services:
9.00 a.m. Parish Communion (sung)
5.00 p.m. Evensong (sung)
Telephone: Vicarage – Morpeth 860242
Road Location: Market Street, Lynemouth.

St. John the Baptist Church
Meldon Village
Consecrated in 13th century

A small but attractive barrel-vaulted building; in 1310 declared by the Dean and Chapter of Durham to be 'a mother parish church'. Shoulder arching of the priest's doorway with hooded mouldings of the east window suggest AD1250. There is a fine effigy of Sir William Fenwick, a Royalist, executed in London in 1652, while the windows feature the arms of various owners of Meldon, the Bertrams, Cambos, Denoms, Herons, Fenwicks and Radcliffes. A unique pair of tombstones, set pillow-fashion between uprights refer to the deaths in 1691-3 of the children of James Thompson.

Times of Sunday Services:
9.00 a.m. The Communion and
6.30 p.m. Evensong alternatively
Telephone: Vicarage – Hartburn 276
Road Location: At Meldon Village.

St. Mary Magdalene, Mitford
Consecrated in 1135

Built in 1135 by William Bertram in the shape of a cross, the tower and steeple were added later in 1874. The top of the steeple was deliberately measured to enable it to be seen from Morpeth and if the tower and steeple were laid flat they would equal the length of the entire church. The roof was burned and badly damaged in 1215 by King John, when he also seized Mitford Castle. The alarm was sounded by the Ancient Bell, sited in the west end of the church, claimed to be the oldest bell in Britain.

Times of Sunday Services:
9.00 a.m. Holy Communion
11.00 a.m. Morning Prayer
6.30 p.m. Evening Prayer (Winter 3.00 p.m.)
All services B of CP (1662)
Third Sunday of month H.C. follows Morning Prayer
Telephone: Vicarage – Morpeth 512527
Road Location: B6343, 2 miles west of Morpeth.

St. Aidan's Church, Stobhill, Morpeth
Consecrated in 1969; Dedicated in 1957

The church was built in the late fifties to serve the needs of a developing community on Stobhill, to the South of Morpeth.

The outside is of unpretentious design and proportions. The inside was originally left with the brick work exposed, but this was eventually plastered over.

The church seats a maximum of 90 people and is a simple oblong 'eucharist room' with the altar and the wooden cross on the east wall as strong visual focal points.

A 'Bishop & Son' chamber organ was obtained from Houghton Castle and placed at the back of the church.

Times of Sunday Services:
9.00 a.m. Parish Communion
4.00 p.m. Evening Worship (winter)
6.00 p.m. Evening Worship (summer)
Telephone: The Parsonage – Morpeth 512041
Road Location: Shields Road.

St. James the Great, Morpeth
Consecrated in 1846

Built from local stone to designs by Mr. Banjamin Ferrey in the Norman style; started in 1844, the church was consecrated in 1846.

The choir vestry was added in 1887 to mark the jubilee of its major benefactor – the then Rector Canon F. R. Grey. The heavily carved oak memorial rood screen was the combined work of a class of amateur woodcarvers at the turn of the century.

The nave windows are clear glass with roundels depicting scenes from the life of Christ as also do the elaborate murals in the apse.

Times of Sunday Services:
8.00 a.m. Holy Communion
11.00 a.m. Parish Communion
6.00 p.m. Evensong
Telephone: Rectory – Morpeth 513517
Road Location: Morpeth Town centre.

St. Mary the Virgin, Morpeth

Entering through the massive mediaeval door, the worshipper steps back through history. He looks towards the east window with its glowing multitude of figures representing the coming of the Messiah, seen by Jesse in his dream.

Most of the building is of the thirteenth and fourteenth centuries. On the pillars are mason's marks and faint traces of painting – reminders of the brightness that delighted our forebears. Their own homes might be poor and dull but the church had dignity and splendour.

Memorials from the distant past to the present commemorate some of the countless generations of worshippers in St. Mary's.

Times of Sunday Services:
9.15 a.m. Parish Communion
Telephone: Rectory – Morpeth 513517
Road Location: Old A1, south end of Morpeth.

St. Giles' Church, Netherwitton
Consecrated probably in 15th century

Netherwitton, 'the lower woods' was bought by the Dick Whittington-type Mayor of Newcastle, Roger Thornton, in 1405, who built or rebuilt the Church and castle. Cromwell's army camped there in August 1651, and thirty years later Nicholas Thornton was 'presented' at the Archdeacon's court for neglecting the chancel. The Lay Rectorship came to the Trevelyans by marriage in 1772 – their active interest has continued since. 1864 saw the rebuilding of the church – a capital and some memorial stones being the chief visible links with the earlier building. A life-size effigy, probably of Agnes Thornton, is worth seeing for her fashionable dress and lovely smile.

Times of Sunday Services:
10.00 a.m. The Communion
Telephone: Vicarage – Hartburn 276
Road Location: At Netherwitton by the river front.

St. Bartholomew's, Newbiggin-by-the-Sea

The town was originally called South Wallerick. After the Danish invasion in AD 875 the town was re-named Neubegang or Newbegining, with several different spellings until we have the present Newbiggin. There is evidence of an ancient Saxon Chapelry here. This chapel of ease is supposed to have been built by the monks of Lindisfarne and used by them in their mission to Northumbria and also on their journeys to and from Tynemouth Priory and Whitby.

Present church has thirteenth century origins. Once the 'daughter' church in the parish of Woodhorn with Newbiggin, St. Bartholomew's was made the 'mother' church of the parish when St. Mary's, Woodhorn was declared redundant in 1973. St. Bartholomew's is in a remarkably impressive situation away from the town, in a treeless churchyard very close to the sea.

Times of Sunday Services:
8.00 a.m. Holy Communion
9.30 a.m. The Parish Communion
6.00 p.m. Evensong
Telephone: Vicarage – Ashington 817220
Road Location: The Point, Newbiggin-by-the-Sea.

St. Andrew the Apostle, Seaton Hirst
Consecrated in 1932

In January 1905 the Mission church of St. Andrew was erected and dedicated. It was affectionately known as the 'Tin Church' by the people of the Hirst. Thirty years later the present fine brick building was completed and consecrated in 1932. St. Andrew's remains a daughter church of St. John's, Seaton Hirst.

Times of Sunday Services:
8.00 a.m. Holy Communion
9.00 a.m. Sung Eucharist
10.45 a.m. Sunday School
6.00 p.m. Evensong except 1st Sunday in month
Telephone: Vicarage – Ashington 818691
Road Location: Hawthorn Road, Ashington.

St. John the Evangelist, Seaton Hirst
Consecrated in 1896

The parish of Seaton Hirst was taken out of Woodhorn parish in 1905 to serve the growing mining community. The church which had been built in 1896 was enlarged at this time. A further chapel was built in 1945 and then the whole church was re-ordered in the early 1960s.

Times of Sunday Services:
8.00 a.m. and 9.30 a.m. Holy Communion
6.00 p.m. Evening Prayer (first Sunday in month)
Telephone: Vicarage – Ashington 813218
Road Location: Newbiggin Road.

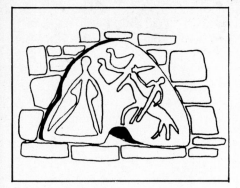

St. John the Baptist, Ulgham Village

The present building dates from the mid-1840s on a Norman site. A relic of this is the carved window head, which was built into the north aisle; the carving of this stone has been dated as Anglo-Norman, about AD 1100. A similar but undecorated window head is in the outside wall beneath the belfry, which was built for two bells but only contains one, reputedly since the Commonwealth. The oldest grave in the churchyard is dated 1610 and is that of Anthony Rumney, Bailiff of Ulgham.

Carved stones at the back of the church, unearthed during the rebuilding of the church wall, are supposed to be the remains of a monument to the Lawson family, who lived in the village for centuries.

The church was originally a chapelry attached to Morpeth, but was separated in 1875, due to the mining in the area making it self-financing.

Times of Sunday Services:
11.00 a.m. Holy Communion
 6.00 p.m. Evening Prayer (1st Sunday)
Telephone: Vicarage — Morpeth 790389
Road Location: Morpeth-Amble road.

St. Mary Magdalene, Whalton

Largely mediaeval the church is particularly interesting for the way in which it displays the evolution of a well-developed thirteenth century church from a Norman core. Steep-pitched roofs have given place to low-pitched ones with parapets. The north aisle to the chancel (commonly called the Ogle chapel) is uncommon: note the detail of its arcade pier. Elsewhere, too, are many interesting carvings in the stonework and in the oak chancel screen and choir furnishings. A benefaction board of 1720 and a turret clock with single pointer external dial, gifted 1796 and restored 1981/2 are among other features.

Times of Sunday Services:
9.45 a.m. Holy Communion (excluding 2nd Sunday)
          Family Service
6.00 p.m. Evening Prayer (said)
Telephone: Rectory — Whalton (067 075) 360
Road Location: South of Whalton Village (Morpeth-Belsay) on minor road to Ogle and Ponteland.

The Holy Trinity, Widdrington Village

The church consists of a twelfth century nave extended southwards in the fourteenth century by the famous Gerard de Widdrington. The chancel with its chapel was also rebuilt at this time. A nineteenth century north aisle replaced the nave's original aisle destroyed after the Scottish Wars.

In the north wall of the chancel are two tomb recesses one surmounted by the Widdrington coat of arms. On the south wall is a large trefoiled piscina and close by are sedilia curiously combined with a pillar piscina. Beneath the east end of the chancel is the Widdrington family vault.

Times of Sunday Services:
10.00 a.m. Holy Communion
 3.00 p.m. Evening Prayer
Telephone: Vicarage — Morpeth 790389
Road Location: Morpeth-Amble road.

Saint Mary's Church, Widdrington Station
The Church cum Hall was dedicated in 1938. The bricks were given by the Burn's Fireclay Company. The building is used for many parish functions and serves a community of about 2,500 who live between Ulgham and Widdrington. The parish priest is the Vicar of Ulgham.
Times of Sunday Services:
9.00 a.m. Holy Communion
11.00 a.m. Sunday School
Telephone: Vicarage – Morpeth 790389
Location: Widdrington Station.

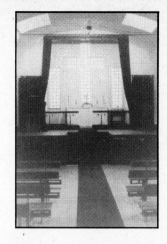

St. Mary the Virgin, Woodhorn Village
Woodhorn lies within a mile of the sea, near Newbiggin. The name means 'a wooded point of land'. It has sometimes been identified with Wucestre, one of the vills given to St. Cuthbert by King Ceolwulf when he gave up the Northumbrian throne in AD 737 to become a monk at Lindisfarne. The church is reputed to be the oldest on the Northumbrian coast with a religious life extending for at least 1200 years. Various types of architecture including Saxon, Norman and Gothic.

One of the most valuable treasures of the church is the recumbent effigy of Agnes de Valence, wife of Hugh Balliol, brother of Edward Balliol, King of Scotland. The effigy dates from the thirteenth century and is described as 'the best and purest specimen of monumental sculpture of the finest mediaeval period in the Archdeaconry'.

A mediaeval bell inscribed 'Ave Maria' reputed to be one of the oldest in existence.

St. Mary's was declared redundant in 1973 and was taken over by the local authority as a museum, cultural centre and private chapel. It is now used imaginatively for exhibitions, meetings, concerts and a permanent display of museum objects. None of this has interfered with the overall spatial qualities of the building or prevented its use for services at Christian Festivals.
Telephone: Curator – Ashington 817220
Road Location: Woodhorn Village.

leisure pool

THE LINKS, SEA FRONT, WHITLEY BAY
NE26 1TQ   Telephone: 531955

WHITLEY BAY LEISURE POOL – The Hadrian Suite – Remedial Baths
Enjoy the tonic and health giving properties of this delightfully modern suite. Use the Sauna, the Steam/Turkish Baths and the Aeratone 'Bubble Bath' as valuable aids to slimming.
Share in this popular social gathering ...... bring your friends.
Ask now for your FREE Leaflet which fully describes the Remedial Suite – its benefits, charges and timetable of opening hours.
Wave Pool, Giant Slide, Diving Pool, Shallow Beach and Teaching Pool.
Beach and Palm Trees. Tables and Coloured Shades.
Tuition Courses – Beginners and Improvers – Swimming Tests by Arrangement.
Light Refreshments, Snacks and Meals.

SWIMMING Regular Opening Hours Daily
Monday to Friday	9.00 am-8.00 pm
Wednesday	9.00 am-6.00 pm
Saturday & Sunday	9.00 am-5.00 pm
(except Wednesday – close at 6.00 pm for Evening Clubs)	

SWIMMING INSTRUCTIONS
Children's Lessons Mon-Fri 4.30-7.00 pm; Sat 9.15-11.15 am
Mother & Baby Classes – Fri 12.00-1.00 pm
Adults – Mon-Thurs 12.00-1.00 pm

Pool and Cafe area available on Saturday evenings for parties – special functions from 7.00 pm

St. Cuthbert's Church, Norham

✑NORHAM ✑DEANERY

St. Anne's Church, Ancroft

Ancroft is one of the four chapelries (the others were Kyloe, Lowick and Tweedmouth) established on the mainland by the monks of Lindisfarne in the twelfth century. Ancroft Church is the only one to have preserved any of the original Norman fabric. The tower is thirteenth or very early fourteenth century and is a good example of a pele tower. It is unusual in that it is attached to the church building. Before a parsonage house was built in the early nineteenth century if provided the living quarters for the priest who was also responsible for the parish of Tweed-mouth.

Times of Sunday Services:
11.00 a.m. Holy Communion (1st and 3rd Sunday in the month)
Telephone: Lowick Vicarage – Berwick upon Tweed 88229
Road Location: On the Berwick/Wooler Road – B6525.

Holy Trinity, Berwick
Consecrated in 1662

Holy Trinity Church is one of very few churches built during the Commonwealth under Cromwell. It is of considerable architectural interest. The church was built in 1652 by a London mason, John Young of Blackfriars, and is striking because of its Laudian combination of Gothic and Renaissance features. The lack of tower or spire gives the church an unusual appearance. The interior of Berwick Parish Church with its arcade of five bays on Tuscan columns and with rounded arches is surprisingly beautiful. The many Venetian windows are characteristic of the church. The chancel and vestry were added in 1855 and there is a reredos by Sir Edwin Lutyens.

Times of Sunday Services:
8.00 a.m. Holy Communion
9.00 a.m. Choral
6.00 p.m. Evening Prayer
Telephone: Vicarage – Berwick upon Tweed 6136
Road Location: The Parade.

St. Mary's Church, Berwick
Consecrated in 1858

St. Mary's Church, a Victorian Gothic structure, was built and consecrated in 1858 exactly 300 years after the old St. Mary's, which stood near the Scotsgate, was demolished at the time that the Elizabethan walls were constructed. St. Mary's served a fishing community which lived in the area called 'the Greens'.
Time of Sunday Service:
10.45 a.m. Holy Communion (choral)
Telephone: Vicarage – Berwick 6136
Road Location: Castlegate.

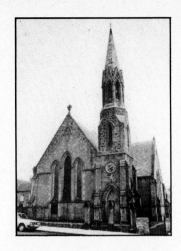

St. Paul's Church, Branxton

There has been a church at Branxton since the twelfth century and its list of Vicars dates from AD 1200. The present building was virtually re-erected in 1849 during the time of the Revd. Robert Jones (1834-1870), an historian who published a work on the Battle of Flodden.

The church revenues were donated before 1195 by Ralph, son of Gilbert of Branxton, for the upkeep of the Infirmary of the monks of Durham. Other religious bodies connected with the parish have been the Leper Hospital of St. Thomas at Bolton, and the Knights Hospitallers of St. John of Jerusalem.

The altar rails are oak from a ship which foundered off the Farne Islands.

The site of the Battle of Flodden is immediately to the south of the church and marked with a memorial cross.
Times of Sunday Services:
10.00 a.m. Sung Eucharist
Telephone: Vicarage – Coldstream 2105
Road Location: Off A697 at Crookham.

St. Cuthbert's Church, Carham
Dedicated in 1790

The earliest records show that lands of Carham were granted by Egford of Northumbria to St. Cuthbert as a reward for his help in defeating Wulfhere of Mercia in AD 675. A small abbey, adjacent to Carham Church, founded by St. Cuthbert was destroyed by Wallace in one of his Border raids in 1296. The hill-top Dunstan Covert, where the army of Wallace camped, is marked on old maps as 'Wallace's Croft' or 'Campfield'. The original church fell into disrepair and was pulled down. It was rebuilt in 1790-91.

The West Tower, chancel and present vestry were added by members of the Compton family in 1862-64. Electric light and heating was installed by Lady Straker-Smith. A feature of the church is a fine oil painting, The Marriage Feast at Cana, presented by the late Sir Anthony Compton-Thornhill Bt, and the altar was gifted by Sir Thomas and Lady Straker-Smith, and consecrated by Hugh, Bishop of Newcastle in 1963. The Arms on the front of the altar are those of St. Cuthbert.
Times of Sunday Services:
9.00 a.m. Holy Communion (1st Sunday of month)
9.00 a.m. Mattins (4th Sunday of month)
Telephone: Vicarage – Coldsteam 2105
Road Location: Cornhill-Kelso Road B6350 (off A697 at Cornhill).

St. Helen's Church, Cornhill-on-Tweed

The church is dedicated to St. Helen, the mother of Constantine the Great, the first Christian Emperor. It was formerly a chapel of ease to Norham and is believed to have been erected in AD 1082 when Norham became the property of Durham Cathedral.

In 1750 the fabric of the church was in such poor condition that it had to be virtually rebuilt. This work was completed in 1752, being reopened for worship on 12 July of that year.

In 1840 further restoration work was carried out, the church was enlarged and the Campanile Bell Tower was added. In 1856 a harmonium was first introduced and a choir was formed. In 1866 the chancel was built in the early Geometrical style and in 1869 the Countess of Home presented a new font.

A lectern was given in 1870 and in 1874 the harmonium was removed to be replaced by an organ – the gift of the Earl of Home.

Times of Sunday Services:
 8.00 a.m. Holy Communion (4th Sunday)
11.00 a.m. Sung Eucharist (1st and 3rd Sundays)
11.00 a.m. Mattins (2nd Sunday)
11.00 a.m. Mattins (5th Sunday)
Telephone: Vicarage – Coldstream 2105
Road Location: A697.

All Saints Church, Duddo
Consecrated sometime after 1870

This church succeeded St. James' Church, Duddo and was the last church to be built in Norham Deanery. Simple but effective in style, it stands in isolated position; most of the surrounding communities have disappeared.

Times of Sunday Services:
Holy Communion (Series 2) 1st Sunday of every month
Evensong (Prayer Book) monthly in summer
All services at 2.30 p.m.
Telephone: Norham Vicarage – Berwick 82325
Road Location: Berwick-Etal Road B6354 near Felkington.

St. Mary the Virgin, Etal
Consecrated in 1858

Built as a *sine cure* within the Parish of Ford by Lady Fitz-Clarence, widow of one of the illegitimate sons of William IV and Mrs. Jordan. Designed by Butterfield, it takes its dedication from the medieval Chantry Chapel that was once at Etal on the bank of the Till.

Times of Sunday Services:
10.30 a.m. Family Communion and Sunday School every
           Sunday – one month at Etal Church and the
           next at Ford
 3.00 p.m. Evening Prayer (winter)
 6.00 p.m. Evening Prayer (summer)
Telephone: Vicarage – Crookham 248
Road Location: On the road from Berwick to Ford – 2 miles to Ford, 10 to Berwick.

St. Michael and All Angels Church, Ford
Consecrated early 13th Century

Ford Church is situated in an area rich in history, overlooking Flodden, and natural beauty, with a splendid view of Cheviot from the porch. The remains of a pele tower are in the field opposite and the crenalations of the Heron's of 1340 at Ford Castle overlook the church. The grave-stones just inside the church are of particular interest, with a c. fourteenth century stone depicting Northumbrian bagpipes and a later tailor's head-stone. Although heavily restored in Victorian times the west wall and south arches and pillars are thirteenth century.

Times of Sunday Services:
10.30 a.m. Family Communion and Sunday School every Sunday – one month at Etal Curch and the next at Ford
3.00 p.m. Evening Prayer at Etal (winter); 6.00 p.m. (summer)
Telephone: Vicarage – Crookham 248
Road Location: Two miles off A697 or 12 miles from Berwick-upon-Tweed on Etal Road.

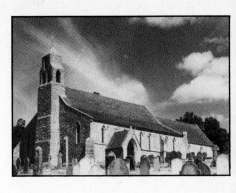

St. Mary the Virgin, Holy Island

Simeon of Durham (12C) speaks of St. Cuthbert's 'Church on the Green' which is now the church of the townsfolk. There may be Saxon work on the chancel-arch wall. The north aisle is late Norman, c.1150 AD; the simple chancel is thirteenth century, the south aisle fourteenth century English style. Copies of the Lindisfarne Gospels and the Book of Kells are to be seen, also a high altar carpet, a copy of a page in the Gospels, made by the women of Holy Island and put down in 1970. The Sacrament is reserved in the old Aumbry on the right of the high altar.

Times of Sunday Services:
8.00 a.m. Holy Communion
10.30 a.m. Parish Communion
6.00 p.m. Evensong
Telephone: Vicarage – Holy Island 89216
Road Location: Holy Island: Turn off A1 at 'the Plough' Hotel, Beal about 8 miles south of Berwick upon Tweed, 5 miles from Veal to village centre. Causeway is tidal.

St. Nicholas' Church, Kyloe by Fenwick

One of the four Chapelries established on the mainland in the twelfth century by the monks of Holy Island. The original Norman chapel no longer exists. It was taken down in 1792 and replaced by the present building (the chancel was added in 1862). The church stands on a hill commanding a fine view which embraces Bamburgh Castle, the Farne Islands, and Holy Island upon whose Priory it was dependent for four centuries. In the Registers (the earliest entry being 1682) there are several entries certifying that the dead have been buried in 'woollen' in compliance with a Statute of Charles II.

Times of Sunday Services:
11.00 a.m. Holy Communion – Kyloe Church (2nd Sunday in month)
11.00 a.m. Holy Communion – Fenwick Village Hall (4th Sunday in month)
Telephone: Lowick Vicarage – Berwick upon Tweed 88229
Road Location: On the B6353 (between the A1 and Lowick).

126

St. John the Baptist, Lowick

The present building was erected in 1794 (chancel and vestry added in 1887) as a substitute for the Norman Chapel built by the monks of Lindisfarne in the twelfth century when they sub-divided their parish. The only relic of the ancient Norman chapel is one of the window capitals built into the east wall of the churchyard.

At the time when the body-snatchers were causing alarm throughout the country, extraordinary precautions were taken to protect the newly-buried bodies at Lowick, wooden spikes being driven into the ground to the level of the coffin lid and iron bars fixed across them.

Times of Sunday services:
9.00 a.m. Holy Communion
6.00 p.m. Evensong (Communion on 5th Sunday)
Telephone: Vicarage – Berwick upon Tweed 88229
Road Location: On B6353 between the A1 and the B6525.

St. Cuthbert's Church, Norham
Consecrated in 1165

Same architect as Norham Castle. Here King Edward I arbitrated between various claimants to Scottish crown; other transactions between the two kingdoms took place in the church. The church has had a long association with the prince-bishops of Durham. Earliest parts of the building are the chancel, the south arcade of the nave, various pillars on the north side, and the foundations of the side walls. Some nineteenth century renovations.

Times of Sunday Services:
  8.00 a.m. Holy Communion (Prayer Book)
10.00 a.m. Parish Communion (Series 2) and Junior Church
Prayer Book Evensong once a month during summer
Telephone: Norham Vicarage – Berwick 82325
Road Location: North side of village.

St. Peter's Church, Scremerston
Consecrated in 1842

Originally Scremerston was part of the ancient parish of Ancroft. It is interesting to note that most of the land around here belonged to the ill-fated Lord Derwentwater, who was executed for his part in the Jacobite Rebellion of 1745. His property is now managed by the Greenwich Hospital Estates. Although the parish of Scremerston is largely agricultural, the village itself owes its growth and development to coal mining. There were several pits in the area, all of them are now closed. Fortunately, the village with only 500 souls still retains a strong communal life.

Times of Sunday Services:
10.30 a.m. The Parish Communion
Telephone: Vicarage – Berwick 7342
Road Location: A1 in village. Three miles south of Berwick.

St. John the Evangelist, Spittal
Consecrated in 1867

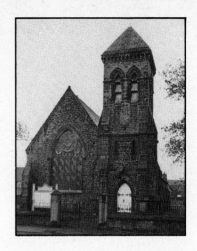

Although the church building is little more than a hundred years old, the church's work here goes back many centuries. Spittal takes its name from a Leper Hospital, which was founded in the Middle Ages. Nothing remains of the site, apart from a street name, 'Hallowstell'. The village developed quickly in the nineteenth century, largely due to its becoming a centre for the herring fleets; and also a fashionable seaside resort with a spa. Spittal still attracts its visitors with its beautiful beach, and the opportunity to see fishing for salmon, still done in the traditional way. Originally the church was built as a daughter church of Tweedmouth, now the parish has expanded and includes three modern estates, serving a population of around 4,500.

Times of Sunday Services:
9.00 a.m. Parish Communion
6.00 p.m. Evensong
Telephone: Berwick 7342
Road Location: Main Street, Spittal. Two miles along the coast road, south from Berwick.

St. Bartholomew's Church, Tweedmouth
Consecrated in 1783

The earliest church in Tweedmouth was destroyed by Viking raiders in 870. There has been a church building erected on the present site since the year 1145. Until the Reformation, the Dedication was St. Boisil (Abbot of Melrose, and tutor of St. Cuthbert) and subsequently named in honour of St. Bartholomew. Tweedmouth Feast Week each year begins on the Sunday nearest 18 July, the Feast of St. Boisil. Present building dates from 1783, with later restoration 1903-1906. Elizabethan headstones in the churchyard. Leper window.

Times of Sunday Services:
 9.00 a.m. The Eucharist (2nd, 4th and 5th Sundays)
10.45 a.m. Mattins with Eucharist (1st and 3rd Sundays)
 6.30 p.m. Evensong
Telephone: Temporary telephone number – Scremerston Vicarage – 0289 6409
Road Location: Church Road/Well Square.

Holy Trinity, Berwick.

Saint Anne's Church, Ancroft.

It's all at SOUTH TYNESIDE...

There's something for everyone in South Tyneside ... miles of rugged and beautiful coastline with large sandy beaches – ideal for the kids and the walkers. Sporting activities to suit all tastes. Disco's, boutiques, and nightclubs.South Tyneside displays it's own history with the first lifeboat, the Roman occupation and one of the earliest Christian churches. It's all at South Tyneside.

For free holiday literature please send 10p postage to:– Peter Gillanders, Press & Publicity Officer, Town Hall, South Shields. Tel 554321

Name _____

Address _____

_____

Holy Sepulchre Church, Ashington.

131

St. Mungo's Church, Simonburn.

It's 3 a.m. and The Journal has just been put to bed!

Even in the calm of a quiet city night there's no rest for the people who produce your Journal. In the small hours they're still busy collecting the news to make sure that your copy has the most up-to-date information possible.

That's why we print so late, to make sure you don't miss a single piece of what's going on in the world and how it will affect you right here in the North-East. That's why The Journal's so important, because it's part of the North-East, understands the North-East and the things that matter to you and your family.

The Journal's your morning paper. Read it, enjoy it —

Have a good morning

St. Mary Magdalene, Whalton.

135

INDEX

(The churches are arranged in alphabetical order of place names)

St. Andrew's Church, Hartburn.

All Saints, the Oval Church, Newcastle (1786).

The Church of Our Lady, Delaval.

NOTES

Photographs

Front Cover: The tower of St. Nicholas Cathedral; the gift of Robert Rhodes, a citizen of Newcastle (1427-1473) and a member of Parliament. The tower was completed in 1448; the crown and lantern were restored by Sir George Gilbert Scott in the nineteenth century.

Inside Front Cover: (top) The rainbow arch of Lindisfarne Priory on Holy Island built in the eleventh century. The Monastic buildings are thirteenth century or later.

(bottom) The Parish Church of St. Cuthbert, Carham, built in 1790 by R. Hodgson Huntley who was lord of the manor. Restoration in the nineteenth and twentieth centuries.

Back Cover: (top) The Parish Church of Etal built by Butterfield in 1866.
(bottom) The Church of St. Batholomew, Tweedmouth, built in 1783 and gothicised in 1866.

Inside Back Cover: The Canons' Stair dating from the twelfth century in Hexham Abbey.

The Editors acknowledge with thanks the assistance of Keith Dixon, Simon Hunter, Revd. Peter Strange, and Tom Warde-Aldam who specially photographed some churches for this gazetteer.

The following photographs are reproduced by permission:
The Bishop: Church Information Office
Cathedral (front cover): Woodmansterne Publications Ltd
Brinkburn Priory: Crown Copywright
Hexham Abbey Night Stair: Walter Scott Ltd.